# SPARTAKUS

THE ITALIAN LIST

# SPARTAKUS

## THE SYMBOLOGY OF REVOLT

## FURIO JESI

edited by andrea cavalletti
translated by alberto toscano

LONDON NEW YORK CALCUTTA

*The Italian List*
SERIES EDITOR: ALBERTO TOSCANO

Andrea Cavalletti would like to thank Marta Rossi Jesi, who provided
patient assistance during the time-consuming labour of ordering
and examining Furio Jesi's unpublished work; and Istituto culturale
e di documentazione Lazzerini in Prato for their precious help.

**Seagull Books, 2014**

Furio Jesi, *Spartakus*: *Simbologia della rivolta*
© Bollati Boringhieri editore, Torino, 2000

English translation © Alberto Toscano, 2014

First published in English by Seagull Books, 2014

ISBN 978 0 8574 2 173 9

**British Library Cataloguing-in-Publication Data**
A catalogue record for this book is available
from the British Library

Typeset by Seagull Books, Calcutta, India
Printed and bound by Maple Press, York, Pennsylvania, USA

[A]nd suddenly there is a moment of inexplicable hesitation, like a gap that opens between cause and effect, an oppression that makes us dream, almost a nightmare.

Friedrich Nietzsche, *Beyond Good and Evil*, Chapter 8, §240

I have underlined many things in your small (but internally great) critical novel, but more than elsewhere, as I can now see, in the chapter entitled Revolution, with that decisive passage on Nietzsche and Lawrence and the 'balance' between instinct and consciousness, where salvation—and we could even say the future—is to be found. You may well imagine how closely this concerned me, given that all of these years I have been occupied with something that could be called 'humanized myth'.

Thomas Mann, letter to René Schickele, 12 October 1934

# CONTENTS

# Introduction

ANDREA CAVALLETTI

On the night between 11 and 12 December 1969, Furio Jesi writes to a friend:

> I give you the glorious news that an hour ago I finished revising the complete typescript of *Spartakus: The Symbology of Revolt*. It's done [. . .] It talks about Rosa Luxemburg, but also at length about Dostoyevsky, Storm, Fromentin, Brecht, and of course also Thomas Mann! It's very [. . .] 'fragmentary': the 'links' are reduced to a bare minimum in a monologue which, all debts aside, resembles *Finnegans Wake* more than *The Accumulation of Capital*.[1]

*Spartakus* is a scintillating and secret book and, without doubt, one of the most beautiful and original Italian essays from the second half of the twentieth century. But it remained hidden for a long time until I discovered and published it 20 years after Jesi's premature death (in Genoa in 1980). Since then, and at each successive reading, *Spartakus* retains for me its singular, irreducible novelty; it remains a book as unclassifiable as its author's genius.

1 Letter to Enrico Pietra, 11 December 1969 (unpaginated), held by Marta Rossa Jesi.

Born in Turin in 1941 (his father came from an old rabbinical family), Jesi devotes his first research efforts to archaeology and Egyptology. He is an *enfant prodige* and publishes an essay in the prestigious *Journal of Near Eastern Studies* when he is only 15.[2] Understandably impatient, he leaves high school right away. He begins to travel; he spends several months in Greece and then in Turkey; he also spends long periods in the collections of European museums (such as the Pelizaeus in Hildesheim), studies at Fondation égyptologique Reine Elisabeth in Brusells, and takes part in international colloquia. At one such, in Hamburg, he meets Sigfried Giedion; they strike up a friendship and begin a dense scholarly correspondence. Jesi's essay-writing activity is complemented by a literary and poetic apprenticeship. Around this time, as a guest of Egyptologist Boris de Rachewiltz, he meets, at the residence at Castel Fontana, Ezra Pound: 'the person from whom I have learnt most in matters of poetry'.[3] In Turin, he founds and edits the journal *Archivio di etnologia e preistoria* and comes into contact with some of the major scholars in the field, including Raffaele Pettazzoni and Vladimir Jakovlevic Propp. But he also inscribes a copy of his Egyptological essays with this mocking dedication: 'If you imagine that I'll continue on this path . . . '. Signs of a change in the orientation of his research can be detected as early as 1957, during his time at the Holy Monastery of the Transfiguration of Jesus in the Meteora complex

2 Furio Jesi, 'Notes sur l'édit dyionysiaque de Ptolémée IV Philopator', *Journal of Near Eastern Studies* 15 (1956): 236–40.

3 Furio Jesi and Károly Kerényi, 'I pensieri segreti del mitologo' in *Materiali mitologici. Mito e antropologia nella cultura mitteleuropea* (Andrea Cavalletti ed.) (Turin: Einaudi, 2001 [1979]), pp. 3–53; here, p. 27.

in Thessaly, where he studies the relationship between Neoplatonism and Greek Orthodox religiosity. He has brought with him books by Leo Frobenius and Vladimir Propp, intending to 'eliminate their contradictions thanks to Jung' but ends up writing a critical reinterpretation of the Jungian model.[4] Shifting from papyrology and archaeology to the science of myth, Jesi now studies ancient mythologies and their modern 'survivals' (to borrow a term from Aby Warburg that was very dear to Jesi)—in poetry and literature, in the history of religions, in philosophy as well as in popular culture—and critically investigates the method of mythologists and (especially in a German context) the way in which ancient figures can re-present themselves, with distorting and dangerous consequences, in settings that have become alien to them.

In 1964, Jesi meets Károly Kerényi, a scholar he admires and considers a teacher and with whom he now begins an intense correspondence.[5] That year, at a lecture in Rome ('From Genuine Myth to Technicized Myth'), Kerényi had defined true mythical experience as the inspired contact with genuine myth (the *echter Mythos*, or *Urphänomen*, as he also called it, borrowing an expression from Goethe), thereby distinguishing it from non-genuine (*unechter*) or 'technicized' myth (*zur Technik gewordener Mythos*)—from the instrumental distortion of ancient mythologemes for the purposes of political propaganda.[6]

4 Furio Jesi, 'Le connessioni archetipiche', *Archivio internazionale di etnografia e preistoria* 1 (1958): 35–44.

5 Furio Jesi and Károly Kerényi, *Demone e mito. Carteggio 1964–1968* (Magda Kerényi and Andrea Cavalletti eds) (Macerata: Quodlibet, 1999).

6 The expression *echter Mythos*, used in a particular sense by Kerényi and later taken up by Jesi, was in fact coined by Walter Friedrich Otto.

According to Kerényi, myth was no longer synonymous with truth, as it had been for the ancients; the immediate contact with the divine, the ancient festive experience in which the community made contact with itself, was fore-closed to us. Images and statues were, for the Greeks, transparent manifestations of God's joy but the figures that today influence the masses do not have a true myth-ical character—they are only obscure, and often trivial, falsifications of myth. This, however, does not mean that myth itself should be denounced. Rather, it is man who must be cured. Thus Kerényi—quoting Thomas Mann against Georges Sorel (the passage on 'myths trimmed for the masses' from *Doctor Faustus*, Chapter 34[7])—opposed his 'humanistic' defences to the most nefarious effects of political manipulation. At the same time, he established a definite hierarchy. The distinction between the originary phenomenon and its false or tech-nicized counterparts involves, after all, a positive faith in the existence of the former. According to Kerényi, then, there are, even today, those—the sole 'true teachers' and 'poets' (like those closest to him, such as Thomas Mann or Hermann Hesse)—who draw directly, for inspiration, on the genuine sources of myth. They are followed, in his hierarchy, by the scholars, the students of mythology (such as Otto or Kerényi himself)—not poets but, by virtue of their knowledge, the direct disciples of the poets, their witnesses and interpreters. These disciples are in turn the teachers and educators of the last group, that is, of the uninstructed or the multitude, ready to believe in

7 Thomas Mann, *Doctor Faustus: The Life of the German Composer Adrian Leverkühn as Told by a Friend* (J. E. Woods trans.) (New York: Vintage, 1997), p. 385.

false myths and to fall under the spell of any snake snakecharmer.

In October 1964, Kerényi sends Jesi the text of his Rome lecture. We could say that, from that moment on, Jesi's reflection becomes a critical reprise and radicalization, at once profound and ironic, of Kerényi's distinction between genuine myth and technicized myth. It is during this period of intense and fertile contact with the great mythologist and historian of religions that Jesi writes two of his most important books. The first, *Secret Germany* (1967),[8] is a study of the survivals of some mythical images in the German culture of the nineteenth and twentieth centuries. The second, for a long time his best-known work, is a collection of essays (on Ezra Pound, Rainer Maria Rilke, Cesare Pavese, Novalis, E. T. A. Hoffmann, Apuleius) entitled *Literature and Myth* (1968),[9] published by Einaudi thanks to the interest of Italo Calvino. Shortly after its publication in May 1968, Jesi's relationship with Kerényi experiences a dramatic and irreversible break. The fact that this is also the time of the Parisian revolt is no accident. According to Jesi, the origin of the dispute lay in 'differences which are above all political'. Or 'political in the broadest or fullest sense' and, hence, capable of affecting the core of the Kerényian theory of the *Urphänomen*. The disagreement between the young scholar, allied to the far Left, and the bourgeois humanist, a friend of Mann, concerns both the properly political character of mythological science and the mythological implications of political praxis. The last

8 Furio Jesi, *Germania segreta. Miti nella cultura tedesca del '900* (Milan: Feltrinelli, 1995).

9 Furio Jesi, *Letteratura e mito* (Turin: Einaudi, 2002).

letter from Kerényi is dated 14 May. Jesi replies on 16 May in a similarly rough tone and writes, in the end:

> If fate dictates that I should be forced to address these words to the person whom I've considered my teacher ever since adolescence, it means the times are particularly dark. I doubt, what's more, that they'll brighten before first becoming even darker—before, that is, reaching the extreme point of crisis. This crisis will probably unfold in the streets and be fought with weapons; a crisis in which even a teacher and a disciple, a father and a son, will concretely find themselves to be enemies, in opposite camps.[10]

It is precisely on that day that the assembly of the Sorbonne issues the call for the general occupation of the factories and the formation of workers' councils. Jesi would soon leave for the city of the barricades. On his return, he would begin to write *Spartakus*, the book on myth and revolt. *Spartakus* is also a reply to Kerényi. The reply of a man who believed in a precise theoretical and political programme: 'to make use of the teaching in explicit contrast with the indications of the master'.[11]

In Spring 1969, Jesi leaves Turin and his job at Utet publishing house to relocate with his family to Lake Orta. He embarks on a period of feverish effort, devoting himself full-time to essayistic, literary and poetic writing as well as to his work as translator and editorial consultant. During the day, he attends to his writing; in the evening,

10 See Jesi and Kerényi, *Demone e mito*, p. 117.

11 Furio Jesi, *Mito* (new edn, with a note by Giulio Schiavoni) (Turin: Nino Aragno Editore, 2008), p. 153.

to translation and his voluminous correspondence. 'Sure,' he confides to a friend at the time, 'my work rhythm is— if you will—too intense.' Between Autumn 1971 and January 1973, he publishes seven books: the monographs on Rainer Maria Rilke, Thomas Mann, Bertolt Brecht, Jean-Jacques Rousseau, Blaise Pascal, Søren Kierkegaard (one of his most dense and challenging philosophical texts) and *Mythologies Around the Enlightenment*, with its chapters on the messianic heresies of Sabbatianism and Frankism which will later invite warm praise from Gershom Scholem.[12] He edits *Archaic Religion* by Georges Dumézil (with whom he enters into a lasting friendship),[13] translates Elias Canetti's *Crowds and Power*[14] and begins a great translation and commentary project of Johann Jakob Bachofen's *Mutterrecht* (Mother Right).[15]

12 The bibliographic information is as follows (using the most recent editions): *Rilke* (Florence: La Nuova Italia, 1971); *Thomas Mann* (Florence: La Nuova Italia, 1972); *Brecht* (Florence: La Nuova Italia, 1974); *Che cosa ha veramente detto Rousseau* (Rome: Ubaldini, 1972); *Che cosa ha veramente detto Pascal* (Rome: Ubaldini, 1974); *Kierkegaard* (Turin: Bollati Boringhieri, 1972); *Mitologie intorno all'illuminismo* (Milan: Edizioni di Comunità, 1972). Scholem's letter to Jesi, dated 1 April 1973, has been published in *Scienza & Politica* 25(48) (2013): 108.

13 Georges Dumézil, *La religione romana arcaica. Miti, leggende, realtà della vita religiosa romana* (Furio Jesi ed.) (Milan: Rizzoli, 2001). Dumézil would go on to write the introduction to Jesi's *La vera terra. Antologia di storici e altri prosatori greci sul mito e la storia* (Turin: Paravia, 1974). As Dumézil declared in 1986: 'Ours is the century of cults. I have spoken at length about this with my friends Eliade and Jünger, and with Furio Jesi. Have you met him? He was an extremely intelligent man [. . .] It is a shame he died so soon. Perhaps because he doubted. I instead have made a pact with the Gods' ('L'iniziato che parla con gli dei', Georges Dumézil interviewed by Marcello Staglieno, *il Giornale*, 17 July 1986, p. 3).

14 Elias Canetti, *Massa e potere* (Furio Jesi trans.) (Milan: Adelphi, 1981).

15 See Furio Jesi, *Bachofen* (Andrea Cavalletti ed.) (Turin: Bollati Boringhieri, 2005), and Johann Jakob Bachofen, *Il matriarcato. Ricerca sulla*

He also writes several very important essays, among which those on Arthur Rimbaud,[16] the relation between Martin Heidegger and Rainer Maria Rilke,[17] Ludwig Wittgenstein[18] and the mythologies of anti-Semitism (*The Blood Libel*).[19]

Some years before, Jesi had begun a novel, *The Last Night*, which would only be published posthumously.[20] A fantastic tale about vampires falling victim to men in which 'Misery, greed, dissolution, fanaticism mixed with pride and baseness, shaped the character of the persecutors. [. . .] And by fanaticism I mean the spirit of intolerance and persecution, of hatred and vengeance, for the cause of a species that thinks itself chosen.'[21] It is hard not to recognize in the persecuted vampires those who were accused by the courts of the Inquisition of having feasted on Christian blood. But the pages of *The Last Night* do not communicate only with those of *The Blood Libel*. 'Perhaps it's no accident,' writes Jesi on that night in

*ginecocrazia del mondo antico nei suoi aspetti religiosi e giuridici* (Giulio Schiavoni ed., Furio Jesi partial trans. and introd.) (Turin: Einaudi, 1988). In English, see *Myth, Religion and Mother Right: Selected Writings of J. J. Bachofen* (Ralph Mannheim and George Boas trans, Joseph Campbell introd.) (Princeton, NJ: Princeton University Press, 1973).

16 Furio Jesi, *Lettura del 'Bateau ivre' di Rimbaud* (Macerata: Quodlibet, 1996).

17 Furio Jesi, 'Heidegger e Rilke: "Zwiesprache" e "Andenken"' in *Esoterismo e linguaggio mitologico. Studi su Rainer Maria Rilke* (Macerata: Quodlibet, 2002), pp. 167–79.

18 Furio Jesi, 'Wittgenstein nei giardini di Kensington' in *Materiali mitologici*, pp. 158–73.

19 Furio Jesi, *L'accusa del sangue. Mitologie dell'antisemitismo* (Turin: Bollati Boringhieri, 2007).

20 Furio Jesi, *L'ultima notte* (Genoa: Marietti, 1987).

21 Ibid., p. 10.

December 1969, 'that together with *Spartakus* I have finished my vampire novel.' It is indeed no accident because *The Last Night* is, above all, a novel about an insurrection, about the battle waged by the vampires against their cruel oppressors, in a surreal but recognizable Turin, all shadows in flight, throwing of stones and brief hand-to-hand clashes, dark noises, pulsing, sudden, shattered street lamps and fallen bridges. 'The vampires didn't carry weapons, they weren't necessary—their savage force surpassed that of the toughest man.' And while the insurgents' charges made the men flee, 'the city revealed its being, now, in the night of the great battle.'[22]

In the visions of *Spartakus*, the Berlin of 1919 is a transfigured Paris. Or, better, in the suspended instants of revolt, the Berlin of Rosa Luxemburg lives in and merges with the Paris of 1968 and casts its shadow over Jesi's city, the Turin of the students' and workers' struggles, while in all these cities of the past and present the Paris of the Commune still shines through. As Jesi cautions, *Spartakus* is not a history of the Spartacus uprising and defeat but an attempt to know those events—almost miming them in the intense rhythm of the prose—from a point of view that is not external but rigorously empathetic. It is a phenomenological inquiry which 'acts from within, guaranteeing *from within* the objectivity of the revolt and of its experiences of time'.

*Spartakus* is a work of montage, at once filmic and Brechtian, in which narrative sequences and vertiginous theoretical flights follow one another and in which the dramatic tension of events is broken, at its peak, by the

22 Ibid., pp. 68 and 66.

awakening power of critique. The nucleus of the book may be found in the introduction, 'Subversion and Memory', an essay published in a journal in 1969 which Jesi later decided to modify and add to the book (as an analysis of the original typescript demonstrates).[23] These pages show, in foreshortened perspective, the unfolding of the work; in particular, they present the decisive theoretical point, namely, the opposition between idea and ideology, between the immediate epiphany of the idea and its ossification in the ideological canon—in other words, between novelty and continuity, the time of subversion or myth and the time of memory.

Already in 1965, in the essay 'Myth and the Language of the Collective', Jesi had reinterpreted after his own fashion the difference between genuine and technicized myth:

[G]enuine myth, which springs spontaneously from the depths of the psyche, determines with its presence at the level of consciousness a linguistic reality whose collective character corresponds to the collective value recognized by Martin Buber in the 'waking state', to which a fragment of Heraclitus refers: 'the waking [as contrasted with the sleeping] have a single cosmos in common, that is, a single world in which they all participate together'. [. . .] The same cannot be said for technicized myth, according to Kerényi's definition, namely the myth that is intentionally invoked by man to

23 Furio Jesi, 'Sovversione e memoria', *Uomini e idee* 19–22 (December 1969): 3–18.

achieve specific ends. In that case, in fact, linguistic reality [. . .] does not have a collective
character, and is subject to the restrictions
imposed by the technicizers.

Mythologemes and images thus constitute 'a linguistic reality that is particularly subjective, like the cosmos
of one who—in Heraclitus' words—is in a sleeping state
is also subjective'.[24]

The difference from Kerényi is already marked in
these pages from 1965, where, for Jesi, collectivity, genuine myth and the state of waking coincide. Kerényi
intended to counter the dangers of technicization by
reserving for 'true teachers' ('poets') alone the possibility
of drawing upon the sources of myth—thereby founding
a didactics and maintaining a precise hierarchy (true
teachers, erudite scholars, common men). For Jesi, on the
other hand, even the most scholarly man was but one
among many in the truly common world of myth. For
Jesi, hierarchies were nothing but expressions of the
extant social order, separating men and keeping them in
a state of slumber.

'Subversion and Memory' reprises and radicalizes
this position. Poetry reveals its liminal, amphibolic sta-
tus—a 'solitary access to the collectivity of being', the
world of solitude and sacrifice—and the poet appears as
the one who suffers exclusion from his fellow human
beings, all of them asleep and as alone as he. But, as the
testimony of a genuinely collective being, this essay is
also a subversive call, an escape from solitude.

24 Furio Jesi, 'Mito e linguaggio della collettività' in *Letteratura e mito*
(Turin: Einaudi, 2002), pp. 35–6.

Thus uniting myth and revolt, Jesi is able, in an ironic and provocative manner, to make Kerényi's words his own. In the 1964 lecture, Kerényi had made mention of a monk in Vietnam who had set himself on fire in order to protest against US foreign policy. According to Kerényi, that act was the perfect example, and outcome, of the most dangerous manipulation of myth—an ancient institution (through which the devout once united himself with his divinity) now withdrawn from its original context, technicized and used for political ends that no longer had anything in common with its authentic domain. In 'Subversion and Memory', Jesi (by then a careful reader of Walter Benjamin, and a master of the Benjaminian technique of citation) takes up the words of his erstwhile teacher but omits the quotation marks, thereby tearing them away from their original context. He too cites the monk's gesture but in a strictly opposite sense—as an example of 'genuine propaganda'. Needless to say, Kerényi would have never accepted a formulation of this kind—he would have regarded it as a monstrous oxymoron, even an offensive parody. But it is precisely in a parodic key that Jesi takes the first essential theoretical step. Kerényi had argued that where there is propaganda and politics there can be no genuine myth. Jesi argues that where myth is truly genuine there are no inspired and solitary teachers—only a true collectivity that frees itself by subverting the boundaries of the current social order. In the gesture of the Vietnamese monk, as in the gestures of those Spartacists who put their lives on the line in Berlin, Jesi finds something that for Kerényi would have been impossible—the perfect 'suturing together [of] genuine myth—surfacing spontaneously and disinterestedly from the depths of the psyche—and authentic political propaganda' [see p 41].

Genuine propaganda is a way of speaking the truth. *Spartakus* is a phenomenology of subversion where the genuine reality of myth is revealed as a phenomenon that is always new because it is irreducible (according to the logic of 'Subversion and Memory') to the time of remembrance: 'Mythical epiphanies are not repetitions following the thread of memory, nor are they the laws of a cyclical history grounded in an ancient precedent. Rather, they are interferences of extra-temporal truth into the existence of those who think themselves to be enveloped in historical time' [see p. 27]. When this inter-ference is enacted, propaganda and the poetic word (the word of myth for Kerényi, and thus for Jesi a word of novelty and collectivity) reveal (against Kerényi, who held them apart) their most intimate and authentic affin-ity, while myth becomes again what it had stopped being since the Hellenic period—a synonym for truth. In the hour of battle, in which the rule doesn't hold and nothing returns, poetry and idea, myth and truth coincide.

Jesi too, however, proposes a fundamental distinc-tion—that to understand revolt as a specific phenomenon means in fact to grasp its difference from revolution. Max Stirner had already argued this, deploying to that end his entire rhetorical arsenal and his vigourous literary style but only to elicit, by way of a response, Marx and Engels' sarcasm: 'The difference between revolution and Stirner's rebellion is not [. . .] that the one is a political and social act whereas the other is an egoistical act, but that the for-mer is an act whereas the other is no act at all.'[25]

25 Karl Marx and Friedrich Engels, *The German Ideology*, Book 3, Chapter 2, 'Rebellion'.

Jesi, though he takes into consideration egoistic components (as the 'space of "pure revolt"'), recasts the opposition in a fashion entirely original but consistent with his distinction between idea and ideology—while revolution implies a long-term strategy, and is entirely immersed in the advance of history, revolt is not only a sudden insurrectionary explosion but well and truly a 'suspension' of historical time. And it is in this suspension that true collective experience is liberated:

> The instant of revolt determines one's sudden self-realization and self-objectification as part of a collectivity. The battle between good and evil, between survival and death, between success and failure, in which everyone is individually involved each and every day, is identified with the battle of the whole collectivity—everyone has the same weapons, everyones faces the same obstacles, the same enemy. Everyone experiences the epiphany of the same symbols.[26]

In this sense, suspension is not a magic spell. Revolt does not replace historical time with the time of dreaming. Rather, it is only in the instant of revolt that human

---

26 The revolution knows no instantaneous epiphanies. As Jesi explains in a text from 1970, which in many respects complements *Spartakus*, agreement between individual experience and the objective or collective dimension of time represents a problem for the revolutionary and may be regarded as dangerous (Lenin) or recognized as pivotal (Luxemburg). More than any other Marxist, Rosa Luxemburg understood that only this agreement, and not the mere concatenation of events, constitutes truly objective time, that is the 'right time' of revolution. This was her way of 'saying the truth'. See Appendix 2 [p. 170 of this volume], 'The Right Time of Revolution: Rosa Luxemburg and the Problems of Workers' Democracy'.

beings live in a waking state. In 'normal time', in the regulated dailyness of work and mandatory pauses, humans are alone, each sunk in sleep. This 'normal time' is in fact nothing but the product of a continual technicization, the effect—as we read in *Spartakus*—of the 'bourgeois manipulation of time'.

The Berlin revolt failed—the epiphany of novelty was interrupted, normal time restored in the cruellest manner and many of the protagonists sacrificed. The task of the mythologist is the analysis of this failure, and Jesi manages to show how technicization insinuates itself into the Spartacist struggle and then vanquishes it. On the one hand, the face of power appears to the rebels as demonic and monstrous, so that instituted power is rightly recognized by them as a form of cruel domination. On the other hand, an enemy identified as monstrous dictates, negatively, the attitude of those who rise up and challenge it. Opposing themselves to the enemy-monster, the rebels *must* behave, at all costs, like humans—they must be virtuous and loyal to the point of self-sacrifice. As the fantasmatic abyss of bourgeois ethics and humanism, it is the monster that paradoxically defines the values of this ethics and this humanism and, in the generous and desperate acts of the Spartacists, it is the monster that becomes the 'depositary of *a* power'.

The negative representation of the enemy as an inhuman being was, as Jesi explains, a burdensome inheritance from the Great War, an image useful to the apparatus of technicization. Viewed thus, even the opposing 'positive' values do not have a genuinely collective character; they are not spontaneous but convenient to the minority of the exploiters; they are vehicles of death and sacrifice that will endure and operate again in all the ensuing mythologizations of heroes fallen for the cause and celebrated in good faith.

We need to recognize and analyse these figures in order to escape their fascination. This is the task Jesi makes his own and which he calls, reinterpreting a term dear to Kerényi, 'demythologization' (*Entmythologisierung*).

Only phenomenology, which 'acts from within' revolt, can 'find a way out from the dead end of the great sacrificers and the great victims' [see p. 96]. In 'Drums in the Night', Jesi rereads the famous Brecht play on the Spartacist insurrection which, in 1960, he had directed (and acted in as the protagonist Andreas Kragler) for an improvised cellar-theatre performance in Turin.[27] At the end of the play, Kragler turns his back on the revolt. Polemicizing with the rhetoric of expressionism, Brecht had replaced the canonical figure of the hero and his sacrifice with a comic character and a comedic finale. *Drums in the Night* thus appears to Jesi, who unexpectedly relates it to Mann's *Doctor Faustus*, as the paradigm of a 'ritual of substitution' aimed at saving 'the humanity present in the German people from the defeat that fortune has inflicted upon it'. Where, in keeping with the expressionist canon, a man should have fallen, Brecht enacts a sabotage and leaves

27 According to Lion Feuchtwanger's recollections—with which Jesi was familiar—the original manuscript of *Drums in the Night* was actually entitled *Spartakus*. See Lion Feuchtwanger, 'Brecht', *Die Weltbühne*, 4 September 1928, pp. 372–6, now in Hubert Witt (ed.), *Erinnerung an Brecht* (Leipzig: Reclam, 1964), pp. 11–16 (especially pp. 11–13); see also John Willett, *The Theatre of Bertolt Brecht: A Study from Eight Aspects* (London: Methuen, 1967), p. 24.

behind a kind of mocking mask on stage. Though it is a true and proper act of demythologization, according to Jesi it paradoxically still belongs to the revolt, to an uninterrupted battle, precisely because tragedy is replaced by comedy and the fated victim withdrawn at the last minute.[28]

As Jesi affirms in a passage with strong Nietzschean overtones: 'What really matters about the past is what we cannot remember. The rest, what memory conserves or retrieves, is mere sediment' [see p. 119]. Therefore, to represent *Drums in the Night* does not mean to rekindle its memory but to allow a past that 'cannot be remembered' to live again within us. That is the epiphany of novelty, the time of myth and revolt which is alien to repetition and memory. If *Spartakus* is indeed not a book of history, the interpretation of *Drums in the Night* can be regarded as its experimental paradigm.

The revolt is the suspension of historical time. But this suspension remains an isolated interval; after its cruel end, the normalizing *dispositif* starts functioning again. Monster/man, historical time/mythical time, life/death—these are actually collaborating oppositions. One must therefore ward off their interplay, which separates and isolates the revolt from history.

---

28 'Brecht's drama overcomes the failure of Spartacism, replacing the misunderstood sense of honour [. . .] with the conduct of Kragler, who abandons the nocturnal drums to return home with the woman who had been taken away from him and whom he has now regained. [. . .] In *Drums in the Night*, Brecht cautions—albeit imperfectly—that victory against horror is granted to those who refuse honor for the sake of surviving a deadly battle. Survival itself is already a victory against those who idolatrize death'—Jesi, *Germania segreta*, p. 101.

Jesi's subtle theoretical manoeuvre, that began with the introduction of the notion of genuine propaganda, rises, in the book's final chapter, to its climax with an arresting theory of the 'double Sophia'—of consciousness as a common denominator between the worlds of history and myth. The I that saves itself from the collaborating play of all oppositions is the one that situates itself precisely at the point of their intersection. It is an I which in knowing itself also 'knows [. . .] permanence and self-destruction, historical time and mythical time [. . .] it is the common element, the point of intersection, between two universes—of [. . .] historical time; of [. . .] mythical time' [see p. 156].

The category of *destruction*, which at least from Mikhail Bakunin onwards defines the essence of the insurrectionary phenomenon, is thus restored to its central place. Once again, with great consistency, Jesi takes up a decisive passage from Kerényi. Elaborating on myth's well-known similarity to music, Kerényi had observed that mythological knowledge and creation demand from poets a particular 'ear': '"Ear" here also means a shared vibration, or rather a shared expansion. "Who pours forth like a spring is by knowledge herself known."'[29] It is in keeping with this quotation from Rilke (*Sonnets to Orpheus*, II, 12), and in the verb *to pour forth*, that myth and history, dynamics and immobility, are joined in the pages of *Spartakus*:

> In the moment that it gains access to myth, the I
> that is subject to historical time while nevertheless

29 Károly Kerényi, 'Einleitung. Über Ursprung und Gründung in der Mythologie' in Károly Kerényi and Carl G. Jung, *Einfuhrung in das Wesen der Mythologie* (Zurich: Rhein Verlag, 1951), pp. 9–38; here, p. 13.

participating in mythical time, 'pours forth like a spring'; it destroys itself in a dynamic process that involves its historical duration. In other words, the I really participates in the flow of history when it succeeds in identifying history with the course of its own destruction and therefore with its access to myth [see p. 156].

This 'self-destruction' does not take place in the final sacrifice, which puts an end to life, but in the sacrifice of the bourgeois components, normalized by the subject in its contact with the sphere of genuine myth. It is the dynamic encounter with a death which is not the simple absence of life but of a true past, a past that cannot be remembered ('the inner space of eternity present in the life of man'). Only in *this* destruction of the self will 'access to the collectivity of being' no longer be solitary.

Now, to demythologize means not to fall into the trap of technicization, to keep revolt alive. Truly to represent the Brechtian drama (the authentic paradigm of demythologization) means living from within an uninterrupted battle. But true demythologization is only achieved with the theory of 'double Sophia' and it is only there that Jesi's book shows itself to be a moment in the battle and his interpretation of *Drums in the Night* no longer merely theatrical.

In November 1971, two years after the delivery of the typescript and despite Jesi's insistence, the proofs of *Spartakus* are yet to be prepared. The publishing house is in trouble, promising but never fulfilling its responsibilities. In February 1972, an exasperated Jesi breaks all relations and retrieves his original submission. At the time, however, he is already forging a new interpretive model, something he calls 'the mythological machine' and which he fine-tunes in two contemporaneous essays: 'The Feast and the Mythological Machine' and 'Reading of Rimbaud's *Drunken Ship*', first published in 1972.[30] Like Brecht, who 20 years after *Drums in the Night* returned to the theme of revolt with *The Days of the Commune*, Jesi, in his reading of *Drunken Ship*, presents a new articulation of the problem of the suspension of time, transposing it from the German days of 1919 to the French ones of 1871. A new theoretical development comes, so to speak, to graft itself onto the same musical theme; and when Jesi redrafts, in the essay on Rimbaud, a page from *Spartakus*, the fate of the book is sealed. The page is extracted from Chapter 1, 'The Suspension of Historical Time':

> You can love a city, you can recognize its houses and its streets in your remotest or dearest memories; but only in the hour of revolt is the city really felt as your *own* city—your own because it belongs to the I but at the same time to the 'others'; your own because it is a battlefield that you have chosen and the collectivity too has chosen; your own, because it is a circumscribed space in which historical time is suspended and in which every act is valuable in and of itself, in its absolutely immediate consequences. One appropriates a city by fleeing or advancing, charging and being charged, much more than by playing as a child in its streets or strolling

30 'La festa e la macchina mitologica', now in *Materiali mitologici*, pp. 81–120; 'Lettura del "Bateau ivre" di Rimbaud', in *Il tempo della festa* (Andrea Cavalletti ed.) (Rome: Nottetempo, Roma 2013), pp. 30–58.

through it with a girl. In the hour of revolt, one
is no longer alone in the city [see pp. 54–5].

It is a page that resonates, as Giorgio Agamben has
observed, 'with an unmistakeable accent of personal
memory', and it is truly 'one of the most beautiful things
ever written on the relationship between the city and
politics'.[31]

While the model of the 'mythological machine' radicalizes and ultimately replaces the Kerényian notion of
technicization, the concept of 'double Sophia' will not
reappear in Jesi's writings. But the category of destruction
will remain central. To understand such machines—
analysing their products, including the mythologies of
otherness and race, the culture of the Right, and so on—
means to escape their fascination and to ready oneself to
destroy the conditions that make them active and effective. As Jesi will write in the mid-1970s: 'The possibility
of this destruction is exclusively political.'[32] In this way,
even in the new directions taken by his thinking, *Spartakus*
radiates an unmatched novelty. Whether we're dealing
with Turin, Berlin or Paris, an inner space is revealed in
the space of the city when myth coincides with history.
That is because only in destruction is time both suspended
and truly passing. It is then that, all along the streets of
the disenchanted city, monsters can no longer be made
out—be they men or vampires, the combatants know and
live in and create a common world.

31 Giorgio Agamben, 'Il talismano di Furio Jesi' in Jesi, *Lettura del 'Bateau
ivre' di Rimbaud*, pp. 5–8; here, p. 6.

32 Furio Jesi, 'Introduzone: Conos cibilità della festa' in *La Festa* (Torino:
Rosenberg & Sellier, 1977), pp. 4–29; here, p. 28.

INTRODUCTION

# Subversion and Memory

This book is not the history of the Spartacist movement and insurrection. The title of the collection in which it is published (*Myth and Symbol of Modern Germany*) already offers a hint about the volume's content—a study of myths and symbols, whose subtitle ('The Symbology of Revolt') indicates the desire to reach observations of a

The first traces of the existence of *Spartakus* emerged in the examination of Furio Jesi's correspondence. The sole copy of the original was then found among the papers held by Marta Rossi Jesi, divided into three folders contained in a single box. The typescript, with handwritten additions, comprised 158 numbered sheets, in different formats (28 x 22 cm, 25 x 33 cm, 30 x 22 cm). The pages numbered from 8 to 26 and 130 to 142 (corresponding respectively to the text of 'Subversion and Memory' and to the section devoted to Mircea Eliade) are photocopies, with subsequent handwritten corrections. On p. 153, above the heading 'Notes', an addition in Jesi's handwriting explains: 'As they are so few, all notes should be footnotes.' In the sketch of a title page prepared by Jesi himself, we read the title of the series 'Myth and Symbol in Modern Germany', edited by the author for the publisher Silva. A missing sheet (no. 61) was then found in a folder with the handwritten heading 'Materials for the Study on the Culture of the Right'. The Spartakus dossier contained instead the 'Editorial Synopsis' and the two hand-written tables of contents which are included in Appendix 1. [Ed.]

general character, beyond the specific references to German situations. However, this does not mean that the events and overall history of modern Germany are but a chance pretext. The starting point and the repertoire of the majority of the examples are 'German' because the German situation seemed to us the most revealing, the most schematic and, at the same time, the most rich in elements from which one can draw conclusions of a general character.

As an attempt to offer a dialectical alternative to the historicist interpretation of the events, this book continues the argument presented in my *Secret Germany* (the first volume in the collection) and perhaps represents the prelude to a third work, according to a schema that would aspire to resemble the one indicated by Carl Justi when, with reference to Michelangelo's monuments for the Basilica of San Lorenzo,[1] he said that man lives or should live first with the dead, then with the living and finally with himself.[2]

## I. Idea and Ideology: Bourgeois Conditioning

In the bourgeois world, it is legitimate to ask oneself if an ideology can be non-subversive. Isn't even the ideology that proclaims itself, or is said to be the most conservative, in fact subversive, precisely because it is an ideology? Disjoined from the context of class struggle, the epiphany of an idea, the way in which it puts itself at

1 See Carl Justi, *Michelangelo: Beiträge zur Erklärung der Werke und des Menschen* (Leipzig: Breitkopf & Härtel, 1900).

2 These two paragraphs partially reproduce the 'Editorial Synopsis' in Appendix 1. See also 'Editor's Note'.

the centre of an entirely different experience of being and behaviour (even if models for both may have existed in the past) are not simply new facts but bearers of novelty. They are subversive facts—symptoms or determinants (depending on your understanding of history) of perennial becoming or eternal return. Marxist and Fascist ideology are, from this point of view, equally innovative and subversive, equally fated to be 'wrecked on the reefs of existence'[3] when the idea, compelled by a recurrent destiny, has become rigid ideology. Perhaps, as Friedrich Schiller wrote, 'When the soul speaks, alas, it is no longer the soul that speaks.'[4] When ideology begins to exist, the idea is crystallized—from the subversive force that it began as, it becomes a paradigm; from the mobile reality that is lived day to day, it becomes a mirror—the only mirror in which the bourgeois can judge the meaning and value of the behaviour of those who assumed that idea as their centre. In so doing—the 'enlightened' bourgeois intellectual may object—the genuinely subversive nature of every ideology is lost sight of. One can, at best, abide by formulae that are in themselves not new, that are in fact usually antiquated; their greater or lesser age then leads one to designate those ideological formulae as subversive or conservative.

Inside bourgeois society, the law of eternal return determines the modalities of crystallization of ideological

3 This is an allusion to the title of Lukács's essay on Kierkegaard and Regine Olsen. See György Lukács, 'The Foundering of Form Against Life' (Anna Bostock trans.) in *Soul and Form* (John T. Sanders and Katie Terezakis eds; Judith Butler introd.) (New York: Columbia University Press, 2010), pp. 44–58.

4 Friedrich Schiller, *Tabulae Votivae* (Votive Tablets) (1797).

formulae, at least in the eyes of those who abide by them. As Lukács rightly observed: 'Bourgeois profession as a form of life signifies, in the first place, the primacy of ethics over life—life dominated by something that recurs systematically and regularly.'[5]

Memory and continuity are thus counterposed to epiphany and subversion. The defensive reduction of the idea and its subversive value to an ideological formula, that is, the submission of the idea to the law of eternal return, which, in its cyclical framework, makes every subversion relative, is a constant of bourgeois society. Herein also lies the root of the *tristitia humanistarum* or the scepticism of the 'enlightened' bourgeois intellectual.

This levelling of ideologies, as subversive and destined to crystallize, puts Marxism and Fascism on the same plane at same time as it abstracts them from the context of class struggle. The non-intellectual bourgeois, the non-'enlightened' bourgeois intellectuals, may then perhaps lend their support to the ideology that favours their interests. The 'enlightened' bourgeois intellectual may grant his services to one ideology or other, depending on whether he inclines—in his 'intimate dark space'—towards sword-honour-sepulchrum or *liberté-égalité-fraternité* (or even 'red flags in the wind'). Since this is a question of choice buried in the 'intimate dark space', there will be no shortage of ambiguous intermediate solutions.

5 György Lukács, 'The Bourgeois Way of Life and Art for Art's Sake' in *Soul and Form*, pp. 73–97 (translation modified); here, p. 75.

## II. Phenomenology of the Bourgeois Problem
## 'Literature-Ideology'

With the objective of affirming the intrinsic autonomy of poets, Rudolf Kassner would have said at this point that the law of eternal return determines their 'false ideas'. Kassner spoke of 'false ideas' especially when he wished to draw from Rilke's work particular philosophical contents; indeed, he almost juxtaposed the intrinsic greatness of Rilke's poetry to the extraneous (ideological) elements that would have been generated and incorporated in the poetic material by Rilke the man in whom was present Rilke the poet. Kassner did not rigorously confront the problem—in terms of *Kulturgeschichte* and even less so in political terms—of the subversive or conservative nature of the ideological formulae that he found in Rilke's work. What mattered to him was establishing whether those formulae were 'true' or 'false'; whether they could be assimilated into the material of the poetry (which was 'true' by definition) or were extraneous to it. In his view, the poet was undoubtedly superior to the 'bourgeois', notwithstanding the 'false ideas' that could beset his humanity; but precisely because of such transcendence, the poet was not even considered a subverter of bourgeois society which, in his sublimity, he instead surpassed. So not only are the ideological formulae of the poet 'false' but also the very ideas that lay at the origin of those formulae are isolated from the flow of the poetry and hence considered peculiar to the man—not the poet.

But the term 'ideology' is inseparable from the notion of a global reality since it designates the centre of an experience of being, in particular a new experience.

Analogously, poetic experience is, above all, epiphany, in other words, new experience and, precisely because it is new, it is subversive with regard to a society founded on the fact that life is 'dominated by something that recurs systematically and regularly'.[6] Even if at times it seems to involve memory (to the degree of giving the impression that it depends upon it), poetic experience is intrinsic novelty—epiphany, not repetition. It has been said (I myself have said it elsewhere) that in poetic experience there take place genuine mythical epiphanies which may be understood as recurrent intimations of a mythical precedent. But this refers only to the paradoxical genuine reality of myth, which, at one and the same time, has always existed and continues to exist for the first time in each of its renewed epiphanies. Mythical epiphanies are not repetitions following the thread of memory, nor are they the laws of a cyclical history grounded in an ancient precedent. Rather, they are interferences of extra-temporal truth into the existence of those who think themselves to be enveloped in historical time. The instant of truth is alone—its epiphany is always the first and only one because it contracts historical time into the reality of the primordial. The rhythmic contraction of historical time is an image that is entirely external to the reality of the phenomenon; it results from the observation of those who no longer believe in myths nor genuinely contemplate their epiphanies.

If it is truly the case that 'When the soul speaks, alas, it is no longer the soul that speaks,' either the problem of the crystallization of the idea includes that of the

6 Ibid.

crystallization (in poetry) of the 'speaking of the soul', or in poetry the 'soul' does not speak and what is manifest in it is, instead, a truth extraneous to the soul and to man (something that Schiller would have denied).

I believe that both ideology and poetry evoke a collective reality, a living together. This means, first, that an ideological experience and a poetic experience affect the reality of their protagonists in its entirety, showing that they are all-encompassing experiences. From the vantage point of this commonality, ideology and poetry can certainly both be crystallized (when they are opposed with sufficient efficacy by a society's urge to survive and by a way of life that would otherwise be subverted by them), just as they can both represent the silence of the soul. But that silence has taken hold because the soul has spoken, or, at least, it has wanted to speak. It is a silence populated by emblems and symbols which are all the more real the more man—the ideologue, the poet—has transfused into them his living reality, sacrificing himself. The declaration of sacrifice and the impulse towards sacrifice are brought together in the will to speak which the soul manifests in the instant before silence.

## III. 'Writing *Immensee*'

The crystallization of ideological formulae—but also of poetic material—is an indubitable fact in the context of bourgeois society and culture. On the one hand, there is no mistaking the historical fate of ideologies which nonetheless contain within themselves the most subversive elements; on the other, we can recognize with Lukács that, in the bourgeois world, the perfection of the artwork is 'a form of existence'. But personal sacrifice is the act that shows how that crystallization essentially takes place in the eye of a beholder who does not sacrifice himself, or who sacrifices himself only in part and with multiple caveats and provisos. That is why we continue to believe that ideology (or poetry) means, above all, living together, even if, in the eyes of those who do not wish to or cannot sacrifice themselves in the same way, the experience and behaviour of the most genuine ideologues (or the most genuine poets) can at times appear solitary or harshly individualistic.

It is true, moreover, that the notion of ideology as a cosmic sphere, at whose centre is one's ego, has been a recurrent temptation over the past century for a sizeable section of European writers; among them, however, that egocentric cosmological vision has generally been countered by the hypothesis of an inversion of terms—the ego as the victim of a centripetal force which, in ideological experience, leads it from the periphery to the centre of the sphere where community is potentially to be found. Configuring the terms of this dialectic as 'temptation' and 'vision' is in itself revealing. 'Temptation' is perceived in exclusively moral terms while 'vision' draws on myth, and in myth—as a collective reality that allows the individual to recognize himself—appears to dissolve the claims of morality. This dialectical process is immersed in history and it is therefore hard to find in the behaviour of historical actors an exclusive allegiance to either of the terms. Among literary documents there is no exclusively moral or exclusively mythical autobiography. The simultaneous presence of temptation and vision determines a mutual conditioning of the acts that are founded on one or the other. It is very difficult to admit that one's existence in some sense constitutes a space of being in which it is legitimate, or even necessary, to write for others, especially to write (for others) about oneself. Vigny's dictum: 'Only silence is great, all else is weakness,'[7] could justifiably be taken to the letter. If writing really means evoking or gathering symbols and signs 'within us and without us',[8] or if from the interior-exterior ('in us and outside us') come symbols and signs in whose epiphanies and presences we are implicated by the act of writing, it is doubtful that one can (independently of its legitimacy) write for others. To write—if one of the two hypotheses is true—is one of the least deliberate and most self-involved of acts; it is the solitary existential relationship of the individual to 'the others', a communion imposed from above or below (or from above *and* below) as a reality that is collectively manifest in the instant in which it melancholically shows itself to the solitary man: 'Why, why was he here? Why was he not sitting at the window in his room, reading Storm's *Immensee* and occasionally glancing out into the garden where it lay in the evening light, with the old walnut tree and its heavy creaking branches?'[9]

7 Alfred de Vigny, 'La Mort du loup', *La Revue des deux mondes* 1 (1843): 497.

8 An expression from Kerényi, in Kerényi and Jung, *Einführung in das Wesen der Mythologie*.

9 Thomas Mann, 'Tonio Kröger' in *Death in Venice and Other Stories* (David Luke trans. and introd.) (New York: Bantam, 1988), pp. 169–248; here, p. 188.

'Reading *Immensee*' is only the symbol of the severe pathos—the courageous melancholy—of solitary writing, for oneself and not for others (or, at least, not in order that it be read by others). 'Reading *Immensee*' is not the dialogue of spirits beyond the barriers of time, nor the fecundation of one spirit by the message of another which, reaching it beyond time and space, would confirm secret elective affinities. 'Reading *Immensee*' simply means 'writing *Immensee*': 'fair-haired Inge [. . .]! Only people who do not read *Immensee* and never try to write anything like it can be as beautiful and light-hearted as you; that is the tragedy!'[10]

Tonio Kröger had no illusions:

The day was coming when he would be famous and when everything he wrote would be printed; and then it would be seen whether that would not impress Inge Holm [. . .] No, it would *not* impress her; that was just the point. Magdalena Vermehren, the girl who was always falling over—yes, she would be impressed. But not Inge Holm, not blithe blue-eyed Inge, never.[11]

'Reading *Immensee*', 'writing *Immensee*', writing, have nothing to do with communicating. They are solitary experiences, melancholy and courageous, entirely incapable of serving as instruments directed to the outside. 'Writing *Immensee*' is like what Martin Buber called 'speaking with God', but though one can 'speak with God' one cannot 'talk about God'. At the centre of this courageous melancholy there springs forth a secret happiness:

10 Ibid., p. 189.
11 Ibid.

And yet—alone and excluded though he was, standing hopelessly with his distress in front of a drawn blind pretending to be looking through it—he was nevertheless happy. For his heart was alive in those days. Warmly and sorrowfully it throbbed for you, Ingeborg Holm, and in blissful self-forgetfulness his whole soul embraced your blond, radiant, exuberantly normal little personality.[12]

Such happiness has its own modes and symbols which furnish and comfort the (otherwise desolate) space of the solitary man's courage. And the comfort succeeds in making possible a durable confidence, even audacity, so that 'writing *Immensee*' can really become writing *Immensee*, and not just *Immensee*. The solitary dedication whence is born 'a severe happiness' is the matrix of *closed* symbols—not of *horti conclusi*, refined little gardens of Paradise, but symbols which in their very structure appear as closed in on themselves, 'resting in themselves'. This is how they manifest their genuine nature as collective symbols, as 'great symbols'.

When writing is the solitary experience of being, the solitary access to the collectivity of being, form is closed in on itself—in *Immensee*, but also in *The Marsh King's Daughter*,[13] it is the serpent that bites the tail (the symbol of time). The house to which the aged Reinhard returns after his dusk walk is not so dissimilar from the 'old house' of Andersen's novella; we discern the common symbol of the sepulchre in both. Andersen's 'old house' harbours

12 Ibid., p. 190.

13 A story by Hans Christian Andersen from 1858.

visible and conventional symbols of decadence and death while the house evoked by Storm 'only' possesses a locked room in which the moonlight will fall on a portrait of his childhood love, Elisabeth. But the ordained alternating between light and dark ('No light yet!'—'It is well that you are come, Brigitte,' said the old man, 'You may bring in the light.') would suffice to confirm the descent into the underworld of memory. What's more, both Andersen's 'old man' and Storm's elderly Reinhard, in their clothes from bygone times, are strangers among the living: 'Apparently he was a stranger; at least few of those whom he met greeted him, though many, attracted by the irresistible fascination of those strange eyes, turned to look after him'.[14]

A stranger—one entertaining intimate relations with death—remains faithful to 'others' even in his solitude. The erotic nexus is an appropriate figure for that fidelity, for that 'impossible' love, since the melancholia of the solitary man can become courageous only if it is penetrated by a form of love for the inaccessible 'others'.

While *Immensee* is circularly closed in on itself, *Tonio Kröger* opens out in the end onto the great outdoors. The experience of the circle—the sacrifice to memory—is completed: Tonio Kröger has returned to the North, he has penetrated 'like a stranger' the house of his childhood. But the novella does not end there—it ends with a letter, which is to say, it implicitly ends with a tomorrow. But let us not suppose that in the tomorrow in which the letter will arrive at its destination, nor in the further tomorrow in which the letter will already have become past, Tonio

14 Theodor Storm, *Immensee* (G. P. Upton trans.) (Chicago: A. C. McClurg & Co., 1907), unpaginated.

Kröger will contest memory, rescind its roots and manage to 'write for others'. There is something prophetic about the fate of Hanno Buddenbrook, dead through his deliberate will to die, after having experienced at the piano the first temptations of 'writing *Immensee*'.

## IV. Literature and Propaganda

The undeniable failure of literature regulated by the canons of social realism is an obvious and dramatic example of the paltry results of the encounter between crystallized literary forms and an equally crystallized ideology. Those Marxist poets and narrators have failed who were incapable of living the *idea* in its genuine subversive value, believing they could grant new health to the traditional forms of bourgeois literature simply by infusing them with the contents of their ideology, now become conventional and dogmatic. On that path, they were unable to produce either good literature or good propaganda. When the idea becomes *truth*, and not a spur to discussion, when language escapes the critical limits imposed upon it by the dialectic of contestation (the limits of quotation, parody and deliberate stylistic mimesis), 'ideological literature' loses vitality and value. Indeed, it is no longer either good literature or good propaganda.

Specifying the nature and finalities of the Proletarian Theatre that he founded in March 1919, Erwin Piscator asserted: 'It was not a question of a theatre that would provide the proletariat with art, but of conscious propaganda, nor of a theatre for the proletariat, but of a Proletarian Theatre.'[15]

15 Erwin Piscator, *The Political Theatre* (Hugh Rorrison ed. and trans.) (London: Eyre Methuen, 1980), pp. 44–5.

The Proletarian Theatre did not hesitate to stage the texts of bourgeois authors but the directors intervened into them without compunction, adding episodes, prologues and epilogues, emphasizing particular statements and situations. In other words, they turned the 'bourgeois' text into a useable citation.

The failure of social realism is at heart the extreme revenge of bourgeois culture which has managed to impose the respect of its formal canons even upon those who declared their refusal of its ethical foundations. The narrators of 'social realism', the ossified Union of Soviet Writers, are children or grandchildren (who have learnt little) of the 'simple man' of 1880 of whom Piscator speaks—the 'simple man' who still believes, in spite of everything, in the respectable goodness of the forms (not the contents) of bourgeois literature. Only if those forms are abandoned—and the only technique of abandonment we know of is instrumental citation and parody—will 'ideological literature' really be proletarian literature, not literature that has been made accessible to the proletariat.

## V. Propaganda and the Language of Truth

'Propaganda' is a very discredited word, almost a synonym for lying. Yet its fortunes closely resemble those of the word 'myth' which today enjoys an excellent reputation in the bourgeois world. When it was uttered in the Greek world, the word 'myth' possessed a ring of truth greater than that of any other image of the real. 'Myth' was true history, truer than the events of the present which, if anything, reflected themselves in myth so as to acquire reality and truth. This could happen because the experience of reality was, above all, mythical, grounded on ancestral images and epiphanies. But even propaganda, in the moments of greatest political fervour, when political commitment has conditioned the authenticity of the experience of life, has served as the very definition of truth. Think of the propaganda of Augustus' Rome against the Alexandria of Cleopatra and Anthony or that of Piscator's political theatre in the Germany of the 1920s, when the constitutive element of the propagandistic message was 'truth'. A relative truth, one could object, limited to the consciousness and experience of the followers of the political movement which originated the propaganda. But such a distinction is no longer valid; today, it is common to be told, by those in charge of overseeing political activism: 'Moderate your speech, we don't want propaganda!'

We would be mistaken to think that this mistrust of propaganda on the part of the activists themselves stems from a rigorous awareness of the relativity of the propagated truths. What we're dealing with is, instead, a fundamental crisis, a crisis in the relations between political conviction and collective movements. Something has obviously changed—even those who deem themselves responsible for leading their actual or potential followers fear that the direct statement of political doctrine, aimed at involving the non-rational components of the psyche (or, at least, the components of the psyche that are usually seen as not dominated by consciousness), is dangerous, that it must be employed with caution, only when it is absolutely necessary, like a toxic medicine.

A not dissimilar phenomenon has marked the metamorphosis of myth. Already in late antiquity, the word 'myth' could no longer be understood as a synonym of truth, giving rise instead to images and suspicions of an illusory reality. The great religious crisis (not only religious but also 'cultural', in the German sense of *Kultur*) of ancient Greece distanced the truthful evidence of myth from the interior experiences of consciousnesses. The personal path to truth—which had opened up and become inescapable for a great number of people on the threshold of the Hellenic period—excluded the great common denominator of myth and its collective ancestral truthfulness. If something survived, it was in the form of solitary evocations of myth—the pathways of individuals or small groups towards the saving truth which could even be corroborated by sudden mythical epiphanies. The true experience of myth, which is collective and universal, remained latent or manifested itself in darker forms—the myth of duty, virtue and sacrifice.

As it registers the sacrifice and loss of the great epiphanies in images that are connected with the ancient religious traditions, the fate of myth comes to be identified with that of propaganda. The myth of duty, virtue and sacrifice gives rise by spontaneous generation to political propaganda in its most genuine sense. And, at this very point, propaganda is facing the risk of becoming the vehicle of survivals that are abnormal, inauthentic, monstrous and culpable, myths that have become deformed— pseudo-myths, since the word 'myth' should only be used for genuine, living myths, myths that have spontaneously and disinterestedly emerged in all their inviolate truth from the depths of the psyche.

In modern times, the technicization of myth for the purposes of political propaganda—theorized by Georges Sorel and realized, among others, by the functionaries of Heinrich Himmler and Joseph Goebbels—could lead, by way of reaction, to mistrusting any kind of propagandistic appeal to the less-explored regions of the psyche. Those currently in charge of militant activism, who in private declare that they mistrust propaganda and only resort to it when they are compelled by extreme necessity, probably suffer from this backlash, as do those who, irrespective of any specific political commitment, devalue the word 'propaganda' to mean nothing more than organized lying.

It is worth recalling that such a sharp break between trust in a political ideology and the practice of propaganda is also a symptom of having 'feet of clay'. Genuine propaganda, namely, the dissemination—for the sake of proselytism—of political convictions which one believes with sufficient intensity to also involve in their experience the supposedly 'irrational' part of the psyche, is morally possible only if one is truly ready to commit oneself totally ('rationally' and 'irrationally') to the struggle. This readiness is obviously in short supply today; very rarely is anyone ready to 'risk one's soul', and not just one's official persona, for the sake of a political commitment.

Given this situation, I think it necessary to draw attention to a time which is still not distant from us (50 years have passed since) in which some were able to embrace and pay the price for their choice of Marxist political propaganda, showing in that very instant that *their* propaganda was genuine, in other words, that it did not rely on deformed myths and that it had become, instead, an authentic language of truth.

## VI. Spartakus

'[W]hoever wishe[s] to be part of the community must be prepared to jettison major portions of truth and science, to make the *sacrificium intellectus*'.[16] In Chapter 34 of Mann's *Doctor Faustus*, these words sum up the attitude of the obliging German readers of Sorel's *Reflections on Violence* in the immediate wake of the First World War.[17] Voicing that statement 30 years later, Mann directed his moral polemic mainly against the proliferation of Nazi pseudo-myths. But precisely in that same year of 1919, in which the novel places the apologias of Sorel's thought made at a gathering of the intelligentsia in Munich, the extreme part of the German Left took to the streets equipped with pro-pagandistic techniques that derived from the reappraisal—or, rather, the renewed experience—of myths, myths in which one put one's trust as perennial reservoirs, latent in man, for the achievement of self-consciousness and the strengthening of the struggle against the capitalist system. The very denomination of *Spartakusbund* (League of Spartacus) reflects that confidence, evoking as it does the name and image of the ancient leader of the slave insurrection, even formally reconnecting the emblems of Spartacism to a seam of German culture that can be more easily grasped, at least for now, in its crystallized moments—in that *Illuminatenordern* (Order of the Illuminati) that Adam Weishaupt

16 Mann, *Doctor Faustus*, p. 386.

17 Georges Sorel, *Reflections on Violence* (Jeremy Jennings ed. and Thomas Ernst Hulme trans.) (Cambridge: Cambridge University Press, 1999).

founded in Ingolstadt in 1776, taking the name of Spartakus, and, later, in the movement organized in Hessen round the rector Friedrich Weidig and Georg Büchner between 1830 and 1840. I speak of crystallized moments above all for the sake of convenience, since the dynamic internal to this current has barely been studied. There is also a different reason. Despite the unquestionable presence of a dynamic intrinsic to this phenomenon, the forms of propaganda are authentic crystallizations, consummated moments, and—which is what interests us most—they attest to a political will to encompass, within a determinate domain of images and moral values, an immediately useable part of historical time. I say 'useable' because every political attitude that aims to employ propagandistic schemas implies a strategy that *uses* a portion of historical time to make it coincide with the immobile time of myth. The assumption of the name Spartacus by a part of the extreme wing of the opposition that split from the German Social Democratic Party at the outbreak of the First World War is a reference to myth, or, to put it in different terms, a strategic crystallization of the historical present so as to evoke the epiphany of mythical time—of the days in which the ancient Spartacus led the revolt of the slaves. In this framework, the death of Karl Liebknecht and Rosa Luxemburg, who remained in Berlin despite the almost inevitable fatefulness of their murder at the hands of reactionary elements, stands (despite the devaluation of their sacrifice by historians like Erich Eyck: 'We have witnessed too many bloody acts caused by Liebknecht and Luxemburg's comrades of faith to prove particular indignation at their fate'[18]) as a testimony of genuine political propaganda,

paid for with their lives. I am perfectly ready to consider
the deaths of Liebknecht and Luxemburg, from the standpoint of the most rational political strategy, as a mistake;
but I want to distinguish the reasons behind their choice
of death from that 'misplaced feeling of honour' which
some historians in the immediate postwar period stressed.
It was certainly not a question of a 'misplaced feeling
of honour' but of the will to use propaganda (today so
close to the lie) in its most genuine meaning—the same
meaning, if we're allowed the digression in time and place,
which in Vietnam is to be found in the choice of suicide
by fire as the symbol of reaction against American aggression. To wage one's person on the border of death while
the streets of Berlin's newspaper quarter were a battlefield
meant suturing together [of] genuine myth—surfacing
spontaneously and disinterestedly from the depths of the
psyche—and authentic political propaganda. Propaganda
was thus the manifestation of truth, or at least of that truth
in which the victims of its epiphany believed.

'We banned the word *art* radically from our programme'.
Piscator synthesized with these words the spirit animating
the Proletarian Theatre. And added: 'Our "plays" were
appeals and were intended to have an effect on current
events, to be a form of "political activity".'[19] The Proletarian Theatre was to function above all as a propaganda
tool, even if its main director (Piscator) did not forget to

18 Erich Eyck, *Storia della repubblica di Weimar* (Turin: Einaudi, 1966),
p. 57. Available in English as: Erich Eyck, *A History of the Weimar
Republic*, 2 VOLS (Harlan P. Hanson and Robert G. L. Waite trans)
(Cambridge, MA: Harvard University Press, 1962–63).

19 Piscator, *The Political Theatre*, p. 45.

mention his 'cultural tasks'. Precisely in this conjunction of propagandistic and cultural tasks—which had yet to be resolved in the direction of either epic theatre or of a mature dialectical function for staged representation—was probably to be found the most significant contradiction in the propaganda techniques adopted by German communists in the wake of the bloody days of Berlin 1919, a contradiction which had already surfaced in the activities of the Spartacist league when Liebknecht and Luxemburg were still alive. The word 'art' could not even be voiced, since it was deemed incompatible with 'doing politics'; at the same time, the promoters of the Proletarian Theatre did not dare (or even think it right to try and dare) to suppress a 'cultural' component and to speak exclusively of propaganda. That's not all. At least from the formal point of view, they still felt the need to distinguish (even if they may have combined them at a later point) between the elements of propaganda and culture. In fact, art had exited the stage in disgrace along with 'all Neoromantic, Expressionist and similar styles and problems, emerging as they do from the anarchistic, individualistic, personal needs of bourgeois artists',[20] only to return to it with dignity under the rubric of artistic craft. After all, the promoters of the Proletarian Theatre were men of the theatre in the highest meaning of the word; they did not hesitate to put their trust in the craft of the actor and the director to the point of taking the liberty of choosing texts for staging without necessarily considering the author's political stance. This meant, above all, that from the point of view of both immediate propagandistic

20 Ibid.

efficacy and of the ethics of propaganda, a man (the director and actor) was tasked with making it so that 'a large part of world literature can be pressed into the service of the revolutionary proletariat, just as the whole of world history can be used to propagate the idea of the class struggle.'[21]

Understood in its genuine meaning, this assertion by Piscator was not so distant from the ideology of the expressionists (against whom he waged virulent polemics), because it was still a question of grounding the ethics of propaganda on the qualities—we could almost say the virtues—intrinsic to man. In spite of it all, this was still the fateful *der Mensch* whose fundamental but mortified 'goodness' was proclaimed, without reservations, by the expressionists (or at least by a group among them).

We know that Piscator, precisely in his polemic against the expressionists, envisaged a kind of acting and directing 'similar in style to the Lenin or Chicerin manifestoes, whose easy, flowing rhythm and unmistakable simplicity produce a considerable emotional impact'.[22] But already the reference to the 'emotional' leads directly back to a 'good man', even if it implies the need to reawaken that 'goodness'; only later, in Brecht's mature period, would the function of propaganda be configured in such a way as to replace the reawakening of 'good feelings' with the dialectical incitement of virtuous behaviour, and virtue would have found itself at least exposed to the ordeals of historical time, since in 'dark times' one is necessarily 'bad'.

21 Ibid.
22 Ibid.

# The Suspension of Historical Time

Marxist doctrine has added, to the moral condemnation of capitalism, the certainty that iron economic laws are fated to determine, within a certain time limit, the decay and collapse of capitalism itself. Unsurprisingly, some have observed that Marx remained faithful to his Jewish origins by transferring the image of the chosen people onto the world proletariat and Abraham's pact with God into the fatedness of economic laws. The comparison could also work with the eschatological outlook of Christianity, if Christ had not explicitly affirmed that his kingdom 'is not of this world'. What belongs to this world is, instead, the Promised Land, though it is no doubt blasphemous to identify it with a conquerable, and *today* conquered, Palestine. It is true, moreover, that the parallel between the inevitable better future predicted by Marxism and the one 'remembered' by the Jewish prophets is, at best, partial. The Promised Land cannot be conquered through a struggle with other men, for that would then confirm its predestined belonging, while the era of welfare and justice predicted by Marxism can only be reached if the fated consequences of economic laws are accompanied by the struggle of the exploited against the exploiters. Marx seems to have been convinced of the inevitability of this second aspect of economic and social

metamorphosis as well. There should be a fated correspondence between the progressive growth of misery,
oppression and exploitation on the one hand and the
growing resistance of the working class, 'a class always
increasing in numbers, and disciplined, united, organized by the very mechanism of the process of capitalist
production itself' on the other.[1] The advent of socialism
should *in all its facets* have its premises in capitalism,
affirming itself in correlation with the progressive and
inevitable accentuation of the contradictions internal to
capitalism. So the setbacks and the out-and-out defeats
of the exploited class could not in any way alter the direction
of an extremely dramatic but inalterable and unstoppable
process. At the same time, the strategy of the working-class
organizations should be based on a painstaking evaluation of the mutable balance of forces which correspond
to the situations determined by the internal dialectic of
capitalism, so as not to miss the opportunities to seize
power when it is possible to do so. It should also avoid
consigning organizational forces and structures to their
certain defeat when the possibility does not obtain.

In brief, what is at stake is, on the one hand, a correct
evaluation of the times grounded in the analysis of socio-
economic conditions and the balance of forces present
within them, and, on the other, a progressive effort to
develop and organize the exploited class, so that when the
clash comes it does not find itself unprepared.

This political orientation, and the philosophy of history that corresponds to it, encounters a grave obstacle

---

1 Karl Marx, *Capital, Volume 1* (Samuel Moore and Edward Aveling
trans) (Chicago: Charles H. Kerr, 1906), pp. 836–7.

in the phenomenon of revolt. I use the word *revolt* to designate an insurrectional movement that differs from revolution. The difference between revolt and revolution should not be sought in their respective aims; they can both have the same aim—to seize power. What principally distinguishes revolt from revolution is, instead, a different experience of time. If, following the ordinary meaning of the two words, revolt is a sudden insurrectional explosion, which can be placed within a strategic horizon but which does not in itself imply a long-distance strategy, and revolution is a strategic complex of insurrectional movements, coordinated and oriented over the mid- to long term towards ultimate objectives, then we could say that revolt suspends historical time. It suddenly institutes a time in which everything that is done has a value in itself, independently of its consequences and of its relations with the transitory or perennial complex that constitutes history. Revolution would, instead, be wholly and deliberately immersed in historical time.

The study of the genesis and unfolding of the Spartacist insurrection will allow us to verify the accuracy of this distinction, and to provide a more precise account of the particular experience of time which we think is peculiar to revolt.

During the first 15 days of January 1919, the experience of time changed in Berlin. For four years the war had suspended the usual rhythm of life. Every hour had become an hour of waiting—waiting for the next move (one's own or the enemy's). These were all instants in a greater wait, the wait for victory. In the first days of January 1919, that wait, which had matured over the previous four years, appeared to have been fulfilled by the sudden and tremendously brief apparition of an atypical time in which everything that happened—with extreme speed— seemed to happen for ever. It was no longer a matter of living and acting in the framework of tactics and strategy, within which intermediate objectives could be immensely distant from the final objective and yet prefigure it—the greater the distance, the more anxious the wait. 'Now or never!' One had to act once and for all, and the fruit of the action was the content of the action itself. Every decisive choice, every irrevocable action, meant being in agreement with time; every hesitation, to be out of time. When it all ended, some of the real protagonists had left the stage for ever.

On 31 December 1918, the Spartakusbund had called its own national congress.[2] Up to that moment, the Spartacists had not dissociated themselves from the Independent Social Democratic Party which, by then, was participating in the Social Democratic government of Friedrich Ebert and Philipp Scheidemann. Seeking to contrast the compromises of the Independent socialist[3]

---

2 Our principal sources for the reconstruction of the events are the writings of Rosa Luxemburg, a detailed bibliography of which can be found in *Scritti politici* (Lelio Basso ed.) (Rome: Editori Riuniti, 1967); and the two fundamental biographies by Paul Frölich (London: Victor Gollancz, 1940) and John Peter Nettl (Oxford: Oxford University Press, 1966, 2 VOLS). See also Eric Waldman, *The Spartacist Uprising of 1919 and the Crisis of the German Socialist Movement: A Study of the Relation of Political Theory and Party Practice* (Milwaukee, WI: Marquette University Press, 1965).

3 By Independent socialists, Jesi is using the common appellation for members of the Independent Social Democratic Party (USPD), which in the original text is erroneously referred to throughout as Independent Socialist Party. [Trans.]

leaders with the Social Democrats, the Spartacists demanded, several times during the winter of 1918, the convening of the Independent Social Democratic Party's congress—they could hope to rally to their positions the whole left wing of the party which was already in open polemic with the leaders participating in the government. For the very same reason, the leadership of the party tried and succeeded in stopping the congress. The Spartacists could no longer apply the tactic previously advocated by Luxemburg in the articles published in Duisburg in *Kampf*—to join the Independent Social Democratic Party while keeping intact the Spartacists' autonomy of programme and action, in order to take advantage of the party's considerable organizational structure and to maintain the relationship with the masses that the party could guarantee. To remain inside the Independent Social Democratic Party now meant for the Spartacists implicitly endorsing participation in the Social Democratic government but without managing to use the party's organization for the sake of the class struggle. At this point, there was no longer a class party in Germany although the actual presence of one seemed indispensable to the continuation of the struggle—that new party would have probably brought together, besides the Spartacists, the so-called Left radicals who had always refused to join the Independent Social Democratic Party as well as a section of the left wing of the party. For these reasons, the first motion of the Spartakusbund congress on 31 December 1918 was the founding of the German Communist Party. The Left radicals, who were meeting on the same day, decided to join it.

The Spartakusbund congress, now formally the congress of the German Communist Party, was faced with the question of whether to take part in the elections for the National Assembly. The leadership of the Spartakusbund, Luxemburg in particular, was in favour of contesting the elections and participating in the National Assembly in order 'to assault and demolish this stronghold. [. . .] To denounce ruthlessly and loudly all the tricks and dodges of the esteemed assembly, to expose its counter-revolutionary work to the masses at every step, to call upon the masses to decide, to intervene—this is the task of the socialists' participation in the National Assembly'.[4] Despite the attitude of the leadership, the delegates to the congress voted against taking part in the elections. To no avail had Luxemburg sounded a note of caution on 31 December: 'We must not nourish and repeat the illusion of the first phase of the revolution, that of November 9, thinking that it is sufficient to overthrow the capitalist government and to set up another in its place in order to bring about a socialist revolution.'[5] The majority of the delegates were convinced that the new party's first task was precisely the immediate elimination of the obstacles to the revolution, above all, the Social Democratic Party. Those obstacles were perceived as so many heads you needed to knock down in a target shoot.

4 Rosa Luxemburg, 'The Elections to the National Assembly' (December 1918) in *Selected Political Writings* (Robert Looker ed., W. D. Graf trans.) (New York: Random House, 1972), pp. 288–9.

5 Rosa Luxemburg, 'Our Program and the Political Situation' (31 December 1918) (Dick Howard trans.) in *Selected Political Writings* (Dick Howard ed and introd.) (New York: Monthly Review Press, 1972), p. 403.

Many heads, of course: the Social Democrats, the capitalists, the military. But always only heads to topple, symbols of power to conquer; in other words, battle, direct and immediate conflict, since you must not hesitate in giving battle when the definitive victory depends only on a test of strength, and you're convinced you're strong enough. The delegates all harboured the conviction that they were strong. Not because they simply dismissed Luxemburg's preoccupation with the nearly negligible revolutionary responsiveness of the countryside but because they possessed the certainty that conquest of the *symbols of power*—especially the conquest of Berlin—would necessarily mean total victory.

In Berlin, the revolutionary forces were considerable. But on 27 December, even before the end of the Spartakusbund congress, there began, on orders from the Social Democratic government, the amassing of troops round the capital. On 4 January, Friedrich Ebert and Gustav Noske inspected the so-called Lüttwitz Section at the city gates, comprising horse-mounted hunters from the 17th and 31st infantry divisions, the provincial hunters corps[6] and the Hülsen free corps. At dawn the same day, the Minister of Interior had stripped of his authority the police prefect Emil Eichhorn, an Independent socialist against whom the Social Democratic paper *Politisch-Parlamentarische Nachrichten* had mounted a slander campaign beginning on 1 January, accusing him of having used public monies to prepare for civil war. As police prefect, Eichhorn did not answer to the Minister of Interior but to Berlin's Executive Council. He refused to accept his dismissal and declared

6 *Freiwilligen Landesjägerkorps.*

himself ready to abide by the decisions of the Central Council of the Workers' and Soldiers' Councils. Even though the right-wing socialists held a majority in that Central Council, the government refused. At that point, the Independent Social Democratic Party[7] called a demonstration in favour of Eichhorn for 5 January, which was joined by the Communist Party. Hundreds of thousands of demonstrators gathered under the police prefecture and called on Eichhorn to remain at his post, declaring themselves ready to defend him. At the same time, there was a meeting of the leadership of the Independent Social Democratic Party, the revolutionary delegates and two representatives of the Communist Party, Karl Liebknecht and Wilhelm Pieck. The meeting came to a close with the decision not only to defend Eichhorn but to overthrow the Ebert-Scheidemann Social Democratic government. A revolutionary committee was constituted, presided over by Karl Liebknecht, Paul Scholze and Georg Ledebour.

In less than a week, the revolt which the majority of delegates to the Spartakusbund congress, by their refusal to take part in elections, had chosen as their programme, had become reality. For the reasons outlined above, we say *revolt* and not *revolution*. The word *revolution* correctly designates the entire complex of short- and long-term actions that are carried out by those who are conscious of wanting to alter *in historical time* a political, social, economic situation, and who develop their own

---

7 The Independent Social Democratic Party had practically been forced to leave the government at the end of 1918, faced with the unacceptable demands of the Social Democrats (restitution of military command to the generals of the Imperial Army, resumption of war against Poland and Russia).

tactical and strategic plans by constantly considering the relations between cause and effect in historical time, within the most far-seeing perspective possible. On 31 December 1918, Luxemburg had noted:

> I have tried to show you that the Revolution of November 9 was, above all, a political revolution, whereas it is necessary that it become in addition and mainly an economic revolution. [. . .] [H]istory is not going to make our revolution an easy matter like the bourgeois revolutions in which it sufficed to overthrow that official power at the centre and to replace a dozen or so of persons in authority. We have to work from beneath, and this corresponds to the mass character of our revolution which aims at the foundation and base of the social constitution. [. . .] There, at the base, where the individual employer confronts his wage slaves; at the base, where all the executive organs of political class rule confront the object of this rule, the masses; there, step by step, we must seize the means of power from the rulers and take them into our own hands.[8]

Every *revolt* can instead be described as a suspension of historical time. The greater part of those who take part in a revolt choose to commit their individuality to an action whose consequences they can neither know nor predict. At the moment of the clash, only a restricted minority is conscious of the entire strategic design (even

---

8 Rosa Luxemburg, *The Rosa Luxemburg Reader* (Peter Hudis and Kevin Anderson eds) (New York: Monthly Review Press, 2004), p. 373.

though such a design exists) within which the clash is situated as a precise, even if hypothetical, concatenation of causes and effects. The clash of the revolt distils the symbolic components of the ideology that has put the strategy in motion and only these are truly perceived by the combatants. The adversary of the moment truly becomes *the enemy*, the rifle or club or bicycle chain truly becomes *the weapon*, the victory of the moment—be it partial or total—truly becomes, in and of itself, *a just and good act* for the defence of freedom, the defence of one's class, the hegemony of one's class.

Every revolt is a battle, but a battle in which one has deliberately chosen to participate. The instant of revolt determines one's sudden self-realization and self-objectification as part of a collectivity. The battle between good and evil, between survival and death, between success and failure, in which everyone is individually involved each and every day, is identified with the battle of the whole collectivity—everyone has the same weapons, everyone faces the same obstacles, the same enemy. Everyone experiences the epiphany of the same symbols—everyone's individual space, dominated by one's personal symbols, by the shelter from historical time that everyone enjoys in their individual symbology and mythology, expands, becoming the symbolic space common to an entire collective, the shelter from historical time in which the collective finds safety.

Every revolt is circumscribed by precise borders in historical time and historical space. Before it and after it lie the no-man's-land and duration of each and everyone's lives in which uninterrupted individual battles are fought.

Rather than an uninterrupted duration of revolt in historical time, the concept of permanent revolution manifests the will to succeed, at each and every moment, in suspending historical time so as to find collective refuge in the symbolic space and time of revolt. Until a moment before the clash, or at least before the programmed action with which the revolt begins, the potential rebel lives in his house or perhaps his refuge, often with his relatives; and as much as that residence and that environment may be provisional, precarious, conditioned by the imminent revolt, until the revolt begins they are the site of a more or less solitary individual battle which continues to be the same as in the days when the revolt did not seem imminent—the individual battle between good and evil, survival and death, success and failure. The sleep before the revolt—presuming the revolt begins at dawn!—may even be as placid as that of the prince of Condé but it does not possess the paradoxical tranquillity of the moment of the clash. In the best of cases, it is an hour of truce for the individual who has gone to sleep without ceasing to feel like an individual.

You can love a city, you can recognize its houses and its streets in your remotest or dearest memories; but only in the hour of revolt is the city really felt as your *own* city—your own because it belongs to the I but at the same time to the 'others'; your own because it is a battlefield that you have chosen and the collectivity too has chosen; your own because it is a circumscribed space in which historical time is suspended and in which every act is valuable in and of itself, in its absolutely immediate consequences. One appropriates a city by fleeing or advancing, charging and being charged, much more than by playing as a child in its streets or strolling through it with a girl. In the hour of revolt, one is no longer alone in the city.

But when the revolt has passed, independently of its outcome, everyone goes back to being an individual in a society that is better, worse or the same as before. When the clash is over—you can be in prison or in hiding or calm at home—the everyday individual battles begin again. If historical time is not further suspended in circumstances and for reasons that may even differ from those of the revolt, every happening and every action is once again evaluated on the basis of its presumed or certain consequences.

The foundation of the German Communist Party preceded by only a few days the explosion of the Spartacist revolt. In the first motion of the party congress one can already recognize—no doubt with hindsight—the gravest ideological and strategic contradiction, destined to reveal itself in all of its starkness in the revolt's failure. With 62 votes against 23, the congress delegates refused the party's participation in the elections for the National Assembly. Rosa Luxemburg tried to see in this choice—which she deemed wrong and against which she had vigorously argued—the almost obvious and redeemable error of an organization taking its first steps: 'It is natural for an infant to scream.' It seems instead that Leo Jogiches remained particularly shaken by the congress' pronouncement, probably drawing from it the conclusion that the party's foundation had been premature.

In fact it appears today that, more than premature, the foundation of the party was insubstantial. The new-born German Communist Party was not—or should we say, was not yet—a party. Its instrumentalization by its enemy, which dragged it into the revolt, met few obstacles precisely because it was not yet a party but, formal appearances aside, a grouping of people all endowed to a greater or lesser degree with class consciousness and the will to fight. When minutely preordained circumstances brought the tension to breaking point, there was no longer a party but a flag of revolt.

The failure of the Spartacist revolt (even the onset of that revolt) was marked by a severe crisis of political organization and leadership. It was a mistake to begin the revolt but an equally serious weakness was manifest in the party's incapacity to limit the extent of the defeat.

To the distinction between revolt and revolution we can add here the recognition of a basic contradiction between party and revolt. The German Communist Party was not lacking in capable and genuinely revolutionary leaders. Nearly everyone in the party leadership was in agreement with Luxemburg about the need to run in the National Assembly elections in order to unhinge the assembly from within and to use it as a tribune to call the masses to a greater and more effective political maturity. Should one accuse those leaders of sacrificing their line of struggle to democratic scruples? To have put to the vote, rather than authoritatively affirmed, the programme which alone they considered effective?

The contradiction between party and revolt fore-grounds the terms of the extremely severe crisis which the party has been undergoing over the last 50 years in the domain of the class struggle. This is certainly not because the replacement of party political leadership with the pure and simple expression of the rebel's will to fight is a realistic proposal. Rather, it is because, in multiple circumstances, the parties corresponding to the exploited classes have been unable either to promote the revolutionary development of those classes or to channel into the process of development a potential for struggle otherwise destined to issue not into revolution but into revolt.

The German Communist Party in 1919 did not have the time to promote any development of the class—a few days after its foundation, the revolt had already exploded. What we need to assess is why that party did not find a way to be (and therefore was not) a party but only the grouping of a class in revolt.

It is not uncommon for a political party to be hostile to the imminent revolt desired by a fraction of its members, or, at least, by those who profess an ideology similar to its own. As a collective reality, a party (or perhaps it is better to be more specific, a class party) can find itself in competition with the collective reality determined by the revolt.

Class parties and unions are collective realities to the extent that they are objective realities. In other words, these realities are collective inasmuch as they objectively constitute the structures of the complex of relations that exists within the class and between the class and the outside. Because of this *exhaustive* character, class parties and unions can turn out to be hostile to the imminent revolt.

In a revolt, a reality manifests itself that is also objective, collective, exhaustive, exclusive. Parties and unions are driven back by the revolt into the 'before' and 'after' of the revolt itself. Either they accept to temporarily suspend their self-consciousness of their own value or they find themselves in open competition with the revolt. In the revolt, parties and unions do not exist any more—only groups of contenders. The organizational structures of parties and unions can be used by those who prepare the revolt. But once the revolt begins they become simple instruments to guarantee the operative affirmation of values that are not the values of the party and the union but only the intrinsic value of the revolt. The ideologies of the party and the unions can be the same as those of the rebels but, in the instant of revolt, the rebels perceive only the symbolic components of these ideologies. This does not happen as long as parties and unions act as such. In the life of the party or the union, the symbolic components of ideology are not lacking in weight but they never become the *only* ideological element—the class party and class union are structures immersed in historical time and space; revolt is the suspension of historical time and space. We expressly say *suspension* and not *evasion* because evasion is usually understood as a choice fatefully imposed by weakness in the face of the sufferings of history while revolt—the suspension of historical time and space—can correspond to a precise strategic choice. What we wish to say, then, is that revolt can *also* be evasion but cannot *only* be evasion.

Participation in the life of the class party or union is determined by the choice of an uninterrupted series of actions in which, it is believed, class consciousness exteriorizes itself. Participation in revolt is determined by the choice of an action closed in on itself, which *from outside* can be seen as inserted in a strategic context but *from inside* appears as absolutely autonomous, isolated, valid in itself, independently of its non-immediate consequences.

The members of a class party or union can, as such, decide on the strategic opportunity of a revolt but that means they decide temporarily to suspend the life of the party or union. Such a decision can be motivated by the foreseeable consequences of the revolt as considered from the outside, in a strategic context—not as an action closed in on itself but as the cause of foreseeable and determined effects. However, because this means choosing the revolt not for its internal reality but for its external one, such a choice insofar as it is made by a minority, instrumentalizes the potential rebels. Whoever does not make the strategic choice of revolt but finds himself faced with the occasion of revolt—an occasion provided by those who effectively made that choice—is instrumentalized. His actions in the revolt are capitalized upon and employed by those for whom the revolt was a strategic choice. Even the rebel who belongs to a party or a union whose leading cadre have decided on revolt is instrumentalized; participation in a party or union does not imply participation in a strategic choice of revolt made by the leadership of the party or union, or even by only a few among those leaders. Party or union on the one hand and revolt on the other are two intrinsically autonomous realities. Analogously, it could be said that the choice of revolt by some members of a party or union (not by part of *the* party or *the* union, that is, of their leading cadre) does not involve the party or the union. However, such an assertion would not be very realistic since, while such a choice could take place without making the party or the union responsible for the decision to revolt, it would in any case—from the standpoint of historical consequences—also implicate the non-consenting, non-responsible organizational structures of the party or union in the revolt. A class party or union cannot be involved in a revolt because their scale, their collective reality, their values cannot be those of the revolt. But this is really a theoretical argument. Even if they are not implicated in the sense we speak of, the class party or union are inexorably forced to endure the consequences of the revolt, if it takes place. What's more, on the occasion of the revolt, their most responsible members are confronted with extremely serious problems and contradictions, in the face of which every choice has decisive consequences for the future life of the party or union and for the class struggle. And it may turn out that, in the hour of revolt, those in charge of the party or union must choose to favour the revolt they did not want, all the while energetically criticizing it.

The Spartacist revolt failed. The rebels did not manage to seize the symbols of power, not to mention its instruments. Once the revolt came to an end, it became evident that, to a considerable extent, it had served the very power it attacked. Not only because in 10 days of clashes the Berlin proletariat had lost a great number of its activists and almost the entirety of its leadership, not only because the organizational structures of the class had ceased to exist but also because there had transpired that suspension of historical time and that release which are indispensable for the holders of power seeking to restore that normal time which they themselves had suspended during the four years of war.

Too long a wait risks becoming spasmodic; an action whose consequences are very distant in time risks eliciting that prolonged and dramatic wait from which subversions may spring forth. In such circumstances, it is good policy for those who wield power to make sure that the excitation of the excessively prolonged wait is released in the desired moment and in the desired forms. Otherwise, the accumulated tension may result in not a revolt but a revolution. In other words, if a release is not deliberately provoked, the tension of the wait may be transformed into organized revolutionary energy. In that case, the direct clash will probably come much later—but it will be far more dangerous, because it will have been preceded by a long labour of consolidation of the revolutionary forces, threatening not only for the symbols of power but also for the actual economic and social structures of the capitalist state.

For these reasons, the Spartacist revolt was useful to the very power against which it flung itself. For that power, the restoration of *normal time* was vital; and only through revolt and release could normal time be restored.

Normal time is not just a bourgeois concept but the outcome of a bourgeois manipulation of time. It guarantees bourgeois society a calm endurance. But it can also be deliberately suspended whenever it is convenient— the masters of war always need a suspension of normal time in order to organize their cruel manoeuvres. Mobilization plans provide for a suspension of normal time and the emergence, as quickly as possible—in a matter of days—of a new experience of time, made necessary by the political and economic requirements of a war. For as long as the war will last, men will be placed in a different time. In other words, they will be forced to have a different experience of time. For soldiers, hours are measured on the basis of guard-duty shifts, the strictly foreseen sequence of marches, the building of trenches and fortifications, the assaults, the destruction of specific targets. The mobile field kitchen (we are referring in particular to the time under consideration, that is, the First World War) with its regular appearances is an important confirmation of changing rhythms. The provisioning of food, conditioned by military organization and the situation at the frontline, fundamentally alters the day's rhythm. One eats not when 'the farmer returns tired to his shed' nor when the workers at the siren's sound converge on the mess hall but when the field kitchen materializes with its steaming or cold cornucopia. And one eats not homemade food, predictably poor or rich, but the food that the circumstances—and therefore also the time—have allowed one to prepare. The time factor is even more grimly determining—one eats a greater quantity of food at the field kitchen if in the meanwhile there have been more deaths.

During war, ordinary time is not in force. For the soldiers, the alternation between light and dark only has a meaning for military operations; you move at night, halt during the day . . . It's the First World War, and the civilians who've stayed home do not suffer these constrictions as much as city dwellers will in the Second—the aerial offensive is in its infancy. But, during the first war, even the inhabitants of the cities and the countryside, the civilians, experience a different time. In the homes of many bourgeois there is a map on which they mark troop movements with coloured flags or pins. They all know that whatever you do during the war counts only in function of the war. In the factories one works for war, at home one lives in accordance with the rhythm of war. Most husbands, fathers or brothers are at the front. Every real decision that matters for the future is postponed until after the war. In domestic hearths, time is measured as it is by the General Staff. And one of the most important modalities of the perception of time, *waiting*, is profoundly altered by the forced construction of things to be awaited and to which the General Staffs devote all their attention.

But when the war ends, this quadrennial wait must find an outlet. For four years one has waited for something. This 'something' turned out not to be victory. It is necessary now to give vent to the wait and to change the experience of time. 'Time of peace, holy night.' Alas, the indispensable holy night is not sufficiently fulfilled by the revolution of November 1919. Scheidemann, proclaiming the Republic from the Berlin Reichstag, was the all-too modest herald of an all-too modest gospel. Neither the announcer nor the announcement suffice truly to change the experience of time. Something more is necessary— every true change in the experience of time is a ritual that demands human victims. Herod entered posterity as a fateful executioner—the massacre of the innocents. But here we are no longer simply dealing with *a* cruel sacrifice—here, at the end of the First World War, the experience of time can only change through a *determinate* cruel sacrifice. Every choice, every action, meant being in agreement with time. When it all ended, some of the real protagonists had left the stage for ever.

At the end of the demonstration in support of Eichhorn, groups of workers had occupied the headquarters and printworks of the Social Democratic paper *Vorwärts* and of all the important newspapers of the capital. The following morning, 6 January, the workers also occupied the state printworks which printed banknotes. Reliable witness reports prove that the decision to occupy papers and printworks was facilitated by agents provocateurs from the Berlin Kommandatur.

That same day, the revolutionary committee distributed some weapons to the rebels and tried to occupy the War Ministry. Strictly of their own accord, groups of workers occupied the railway stations. While the battle waged almost incessantly in the streets, the revolutionary committee spent long hours in meetings—after exhausting debates, the members of the committee reached the conclusion that it was necessary to negotiate with their adversary. Contemporaneously, in Düsseldorf and Bremen, the workers' and soldiers' councils seized power while in the Rhineland counter-revolutionary troops were defeated in open battle. In Berlin, however, thousands of working-class fighters sacrificed themselves in the defence of strategic positions which—given how the fight had been led—could not be held for long (and

Berlin represented, from every point of view, the hard core of the class struggle). On the night between 8 and 9 January, the counter-revolutionary troops set their machine-gun fire on the editorial offices of *Rote Fahne* on Wilhelmstrasse and attempted an assault, which was then postponed for (unwarranted) fear of a trap. On the 9th, the offices were abandoned. The evening of 10 January, while negotiations were continuing between the Social Democratic government and that part of the Independent Social Democratic Party which had opted for revolt, the Berlin Kommandatur, with a swift strike, managed to arrest a number of Independent socialist and communist leaders, among them Georg Ledebour and Ernst Meyer. Ledebour was, in fact, one of the delegates at the negotiations. At dawn on 11 January those negotiations ended, as vainly as they began. During the same hours there began the heavy shelling of the offices of *Vorwärts* occupied by the workers. They repelled an initial attack by the troops; but after two more hours of gunfire, the 300 survivors were forced to accept an unconditional surrender. The troops demolished the headquarters of the Communist Party on Friedrichstrasse and arrested Leo Jogiches and Hugo Eberlein. That evening a meeting took place, in the presence of Liebknecht, in the apartment close to Halle Gate where Luxemburg had taken refuge after leaving the editorial offices of *Rote Fahne*. Because this area was now at the centre of the clashes, Liebknecht and Luxemburg left right away to stay with a family in the working-class neighbourhood of Neukölln, where counter-revolutionary troops did not yet dare enter in force. Meanwhile, all the parliamentarians (bar one) seized before the surrender of the workers occupying the *Vorwärts* had been killed. On 13 January, a report—most probably false—led Liebknecht and Luxemburg to leave their relatively safe dwelling in Neukölln to stay with friends in Wilmersdorf. They had vehemently refused to seek shelter in Frankfurt—an entreaty they received from all quarters. In Wilmersdorf, Liebknecht and Luxemburg drafted some articles with the aim of 'drawing the balance sheet of what happened, to evaluate the events and their results in light of the great standard of history'. At nine in the evening on 15 January, Liebknecht, Luxemburg and Pieck were arrested in their hiding place and led to the Hotel Eden. A few hours later, the corpse of Liebknecht was taken—as the body of an unknown person—to an emergency ward; Luxemburg's body was thrown from the Liechtenstein bridge into the Landwehr canal from which it resurfaced five months later. The revolt continued to suspend historical time— during the spring of 1919 the legend made the rounds in the working-class neighbourhoods of Berlin that Luxemburg had not been killed, that she had escaped the troops and, when the hour sounded, would once again return at the head of the fighters, leading them to victory.

# The Symbols of Power

When Josephus, son of Matthias (the future Flavius Josephus), was a commander of Galilee and of the province of Gamla, he tried to consolidate the Jewish resistance against the Romans by organizing the insurgent troops according to the same schemas as the occupying army. With far fewer reasons, the organizations of the working class have long taken the structures of their adversary as their model. Class parties and unions are subject to the indisputable power of fascination exerted by their capitalist counterpart, and they strive to counter it by transforming themselves into organs that are basically similar to those that characterize capitalism. We are not dealing simply with a strategic choice which may be more or less acceptable. One of the most fearsome conquests of capitalism consists in having conferred a *symbolic* value of strength and power to its structures—a symbolic value whose recognition is not escaped even by many of those who aim to bring capitalism down. It was not by chance that Marx affirmed—though in a positive sense—that the premises of socialism are to be found in capitalism. In a vast number of cases, the institutions of capitalism appear to the exploited as non-contingent symbols of power.

Even if one recognizes that determinate symbols of power belong to the enemy, one is still exposed to the temptation to believe that those symptoms are in any case—by a kind of non-contingent objectivity—symbols of strength, and that they must therefore be taken possession of in order to win the battle.

There are close ties between the genesis and triggering of phenomena of spontaneous insurrection on the one hand and the various forms taken by the symbols of power on the other. Firstly, those symbols constitute the face of the enemy against whom one rises up—a face that may turn, in various ways, into such a provocation that it can end up determining the very movement of the insurrectionary mechanism. We should not forget, however, that a spontaneous insurrection is never *only* an insurrection *against someone*. In the phenomenon of spontaneous insurrection (we understand by spontaneous insurrection also a revolt like the Spartacist one—spontaneous but doubtless triggered by a slogan coming from those who responded to the provocation and to the urge to rebel and became its spokespeople), a role is played by the urge to rebel for the sake of rebelling, independently of the face or nature of the enemy. It is true that the 'irrational' urges to rebel for the sake of rebelling remain the intimate prerogative of the exploited and oppressed, and seem aptly to reflect their material situation (leading to the formulation of a simple framework of cause and effect). We believe, however, that the condition imposed upon workers by the capitalist system is not the *only* (and reasonable) impetus to rebel. In the phenomenon of spontaneous insurrection are also present numerous elements of rebellion born from 'private' individual frustrations, alien to the framework of class consciousness and class struggle, as well as the impulse of individuals to benefit from the experience of collective force, the force of the group. All the more so in that insurrection, immediately channelled into the ambit of class struggle and enriched by the becoming-conscious of ideal motives, represents for the individual the possibility to vanquish his love-hatred for the mass and to melt into it, overcoming 'for the cause' and, in the momentum of fighting 'for the cause', the inevitable obstacles and sacrifices imposed by participation in and devotion to the group.

This space of 'pure revolt', which we deem to be present in every spontaneous insurrection, certainly existed in the Berlin revolt of January 1919. More, it was the looming presence of definite enemy faces—the lords of war, the lords of money, the traitors of the working class—which favoured the strengthening of that urge to 'pure revolt'. The targets of the insurrection tended, in fact, to delineate themselves clearly within the ambit of symbols and pseudo-myths—it was easy to think of rising up not so much against a concrete political and economic situation ('technical insurrection') as against some hideous adversaries, less than human in their moral traits, more than human in their physical-symbolic features. It was easy, in brief, to think of rising up against 'monsters'—this constitutes but an embryonically rationalized form of rebelling for the sake of rebelling.

The recently concluded war had also contributed to the maturing of such a situation. During the First World War, the peculiar nature of the struggle had often placed the combatants in the conditions of those who are facing not an equal adversary but a 'monster'. The characteristics of trench warfare, which obliged soldiers to long stays in a particularly hideous and inhuman context, the kind of weapons employed (for the first time artillery took on such an important role, not to mention unusual weapons like gas), the fire from every direction including the sky, the gases that attacked in an unprecedented way and demanded the 'loss of the face' from those forced to defend themselves with masks (from Karl Kraus to Wolfgang Borchert, that is, until the end of the Second World War, the horror of men 'without a face', of perambulating gas masks, is symptomatic)—all this led everyone to see themselves as engaged in a war against 'monsters', different from the wars of past, however gruesome those may have been, different, that is, from 'wars between men'.

All the enemy propaganda that insisted on attributing to the central empires not only responsibility for the war but a blacker moral stain than usually attaches to the instigators of wars, also played its part. At the end of the war, the Germans were no longer immune from that work of persuasion which was based on depicting war as a contest between the defenders of civilization and barbarism-Germanism. Many studies have already dealt with the way in which this situation was entangled with the genesis of Nazism. We should not forget, however, that those who rose up in Berlin in January 1919 also belonged to the same German people who had been incessantly accused of barbarism. Despite the total extraneousness to German nationalism of the leaders of Spartacism, we can presume that those German workers who were most conscious of the social background of the war, readier to consider French, English and Russian soldiers as comrades subject to the same exploitation (in this case, martial rather than industrial), must have experienced the impact of anti-German propaganda—at least unconsciously. That's why their insurrection against the kaiser, against the lords of war or their friends and accomplices, the lords of money, was—aside from a precise episode in the class struggle—a liberating release. Rising up also meant 'not being German', in the sense of 'bearers of barbarism', 'criminals par excellence'. At a rational level, most Spartacists will never have felt united with those who truly represented Germany at war; but it cannot be denied that—as we said, at least unconsciously—enemy propaganda had in some sense also affected them, further arousing in the immediate postwar period the urge to free themselves from the condition of being 'Germans', to rebel. Moreover, the rational elaborations of that psychological disquiet contributed to seeing in the masters of Germany not only the exploiters—the bosses coldly considered—but also the pseudo-mythical prototypes of the 'monsters' (and, as we already noted, the war rendered the hideous awareness of 'monsters' more frequent).

Those 'monsters' were the repositories of power, faces of power. The scene of the popular pseudo-insurrection neutralized by the prestige of Consul Buddenbrook could no longer be repeated in any way. Not only because of the further maturing of class consciousness and the organization of the labouring forces but also because the war had forcefully placed the bosses in the category of 'monsters'.

In the Spartacist insurrection, this component played a determining role. Fighting through the dark and wintry streets of Berlin was also fighting against the 'monsters of the night'. The spontaneity with which the provocation was welcomed and the revolt chosen was also born from this substrate. In those years—and already in the prewar period—the figure of the industrial autocrat had revealed itself as identical to that of the lord of war. In industrial districts outside the great cities, the boss who lived in the villa dominating the factories and the workers' houses, who meted out punishment but sent his wife to bring gifts for newborns, was really the 'lord and master' of traditional symbolic forms. In the great urban centres, though the subjection remained the same, the features of the 'feudal group' were rarer; offsetting this, the very structure of great conurbations, the 'menacing city' built by and for the bosses—above all, the grim reality of Berlin real estate—made the horror of the symbols of power *ex alto* loom physically over the exploited class in every hour and action of their lives. This is where, especially in Germany, we find not the birth but the first great experience of the city as the hell of the multitudes. In a kind of literary harmony, a battle was fought through the freezing and darkened city (Berlin) that represented a different version, adapted to the times, of the struggle of the Parisian Commune. Not a city—like Paris had been—occupied and used, its bourgeois values deconsecrated, by a people besieged; but the city that opposes its granitic symbols as a 'city of the boss' to those who fight against the citizen bosses, against the *bosses of the city*. Not by chance, shortly before the war, Georg Heym conjured up in his poems the 'demons of the city'. During the

Spartacist revolt, even when there is fighting at intersections, the city is the true nocturnal and snowy 'hell'—in nothing does this city, built by the bosses, show its solidarity with the rebels. It is the looming, stony symbol of the 'monsters' who will soon prevail.

That 'demythologization' whose necessity has been particularly noted over the past few decades in the fields of philosophy and religion still remains at the margins (if not entirely outside) of the ideological problems of the exploited class. The organizations of this class, parties or unions, have yet to understand how necessary it is for their reality to present its own structures rather than the ones imitated from the rival class. The collective organized realities of the exploited become ever less collective, to the degree that they imitate the structures proper to the class of the exploiters. Class consciousness is not just consciousness of the economic relations that determine classist differentiation, it is also consciousness of the human experience that characterizes belonging to the class of the exploited.

We have said 'demythologization' and not 'demystification'. The human experience of the exploited classes also fatefully corresponds to the epiphany of determinate mythic images. It is not a question of trying, pointlessly, to suppress them; rather, it is a matter of acting critically in the course of the maturing of class consciousness to free the exploited from the power of fascination of myths belonging to the exploiters. The latter are indeed false myths, non-genuine myths for the exploited, but they exercise the dangerous power of effective myths. It is also a matter of preventing the genuine myths of the exploited class from giving rise to a mythological system that would then serve as the ground for the strategy of political organizations. Genuine myths can serve as a unifying element, a collective reality, a common language. But using such myths to ground a strategy of struggle means imitating the adversary and his strategic behaviour. The scanty attention devoted to this determining element in the Marxist analysis of capitalism seems to us to be one of its most serious weaknesses. It was not the great theorists of Marxism but the last great representatives of bourgeois culture who shed light, often with great candour, on the relationship between myth and the strategies of struggle typical of capitalism, a relationship so deeply rooted and developed as to make the analogous relationship within the exploited class look like a very pale imitation. It is symptomatic that the major elucidations of this state of affairs come not so much from economists, sociologists or philosophers as from the last and highest bourgeois exponents of literary art. It is also symptomatic that the most enlightening among these testimonies are in the German language. But not in Max Weber or Werner Sombart, or even Max Scheler, but in Theodor Storm and Thomas Mann.

In *The Lion's Meal*, François de Curel poses an almost 'Engelsian' question, which can be phrased as follows: Does a man of worth, very wealthy and set on devoting himself to the happiness of the working class, make himself more useful by committing his eloquence to social service or by becoming a great industrialist, profiting no doubt but giving a livelihood to many men round him, so that they may satisfy their needs?[1] It is in this second sense—a character in the comedy concludes—that such a man can truly make himself useful, provided he is intelligent and energetic. The majority of men needs to have their ideas and actions suggested to them; the individual who knows how to force himself upon the mass and dictate its movements is the benefactor of humanity.

To approach this attitude with irony would be inappropriate. It would mean avoiding a singular node in the bourgeois consciousness and European culture of the first years of the twentieth century—just consider that the historical figure that is most 'sympathetically' bound if not to François de Curel then at least to one of his closest pupils, Marie Lenéru, was Saint-Just.[2] And we cannot avoid here a discussion of Maurice Barrès, that great admirer and advocate of Lenéru's essay on Saint-Just. If it is possible today to feel the temptation of irony when considering *The Lion's Meal*, it is doubtful that any ironic reflex can be elicited by a work as gloomy (which is not to say it is of little literary value) as *The Sacred Hill*, which Barrès wrote on the eve of the First World War.[3] The ending of the novel, the conversion and death of Léopold Baillard (the priest already in revolt against the Church) and the dialogue between *Prairie* and *Chapelle*,[4] which concludes with the victory of the *Chapelle* as both rule and hierarchical order—thus also satisfying the individualism of the rebel—provide a rather enlightening testimony about the precise relationship between myth and political strategy peculiar to the bourgeoisie. Not so much in themselves

1 François de Curel, *Le Repas du Lion* (1897).

2 Marie Lenéru, *Essai sur Saint-Just* (Paris: Grasset, 'Cahiers verts', 1922).

3 Maurice Barrès, *La colline inspirée* (Paris: Emil-Paul Frères, 1913).

4 Respectively, the symbols of heretical revolt and the traditional Church.

as in the context of the spiritual vicissitudes of Barrès, who had been a Boulangist, an anti-Dreyfusard, a defender of nationalist and religious tradition. They offer space and 'sympathy' to the revolt, recognizing not only its termination but also its fulfilment in the experience of the myths to which power conjoins itself and in the acceptance of the symbols that emanate from power. The Saint-Just that Barrès could appreciate enthusiastically was a character—of doubtful historical veracity—to which Luxemburg's previously quoted words about bourgeois revolutions are perfectly suited: 'When it sufficed to overthrow the central power and put in its place one or a couple of dozen new men.'

Yet there is much greater depth and insight in the testimony of he who at the time of the First World War could have been viewed more or less as the German equivalent of Barrès, namely, Mann. About 10 years before Barrès wrote *The Sacred Hill*, Mann had provided, in *Buddenbrooks*, the most conscious and elevated demonstration of the moral groundwork—and not simply the efficacy—of the value of the symbols of power in bourgeois society as well as of their genesis in the intimate relationship between myth and political strategy (in *The Sacred Hill* it is, above all, the *efficacy* of the symbols of power that is at stake).[5] In *Buddenbrooks*, the richest and most complete figure, the most historically true as a symbol—as well as most artistically accomplished—is that of Consul Jean. It already contains, with even greater clarity, everything that Mann would later write in the chapter 'Spirit of the

5 Thomas Mann, *Buddenbrooks* (Helen Tracy Lowe-Porter trans.) (New York: Alfred A. Knopf, 1930).

Bourgeoisie' in *Reflections of a Nonpolitical Man*. In the figure of Consul Jean, the lucidity of philosophical speculation and the depth of political experience acquire—in a way perhaps unmatched in the rest of Mann's works—the clarity of poetry.[6]

It is the poetic quality itself which transforms representational techniques into an experience of being that makes the figure of Consul Jean Buddenbrook truer than Weber's or Sombart's 'capitalist', and demonstrates that Ludwig Pohle's famous assertion—'Capitalism could be defined, on the basis of its origin, as the current economic organization seen through the lenses of socialism'[7]—does not sufficiently take into account how the 'current economic organization' appeared through the lenses of the last great members of the bourgeoisie. We deliberately mentioned Theodor Storm as among the most significant observers of the relationship between myth and bourgeois political strategy so as to not limit our discussion of these testimonies to a writer like Mann, born only 12 years before Marx's death. 'I could go to extremes without any fear of losing myself,' Storm wrote. This phrase, seized upon by the young Lukács,[8] could be used as the epigram for a discussion of the symbols of power in bourgeois civilization—not so much because of its anticipation of Nietzsche as for how it implicitly affirms a 'moral strategy' on mythical foundations. It is no longer Calvin, but nothing short of the pre-Christian substrate of Germanism,

6 Thomas Mann, *Reflections of a Nonpolitical Man* (W. D. Morris trans.) (New York: Ungar, 1983).

7 Ludwig Pohle, 'Kapitalismus' in *Handwörterbuch der Staatswissenschaften*, VOL. 5, 4th edn (Jena, 1923), p. 584.

8 Lukács, 'The Bourgeois Way of Life' in *Soul and Form*, p. 77.

which intervenes here in the definition of a morality that entertains close relations both with the 'perfection of the artwork as a form of existence' and with death—the two poles between which Storm struggled throughout his existence. Let us quote Lukács: 'A bourgeois profession as a form of life signifies, in the first place, the primacy of ethics in life—life dominated by something that recurs systematically and regularly.'[9] Myth can indeed become the foundation of political strategy if the relationship between acting and dying is consciously configured and realized in the recognition of an eternal return. On multiple occasions, Mann underlined the anti-Christian components in Storm's work, how it drew on a remote Germanic and Baltic paganism. This substrate, which is dominated by a far gloomier (which is not to say falser) eternal return than that of Christian eschatology, is, if not the true historical determinant then at least the fitting emblem of a historical determinant far deeper than Calvinist Christianity in the genesis of the bourgeois use of myth as a foundation for political strategy. We have already noted how symptomatic it is that the most enlightening testimonies about the symbols of bourgeois power are formulated in the German language. The pre-Christian and anti-Christian Middle Ages always played a determining role in the consciousness and the regrets of German bourgeois civilization, in the nationalism of Theodor Storm and Ludwig Uhland but also in that emblematic pietism that reaches all the way back to *Werther*. The hidden thread that connects *Werther* to *Immensee* and *Immensee* to *Tonio Kröger* is this singular fascination of the abyss of history also

9 Ibid., p. 75.

regarded as the historical abyss of ethics; it is from this same perspective that one should gauge the impact of Germanic speculations on natural right (not only in the domain of the philosophy of history). The pre-Christian Middle Ages must be understood here as simultaneously symbol and myth—not as a 'historical fact'. It is a mannered Middle Ages, if you will. But taking this as warrant to deny the weight of what hides itself behind its emblem would be as naive as considering untrustworthy—and therefore not very meaningful!—the characters of the Wagnerian Middle Ages.

'What hides itself behind its emblem'—it is not so difficult to give it a seemingly more precise name. It is remarkable how little has been made in exegeses of *Doctor Faustus* of the very close relation between Adrian Leverkühn's conversation with the Devil and Ivan Karamazov's analogous conversation;[10] all the more remarkable in that the formal similarities alone are very evident. But an explanation can perhaps be furnished by Hans Mayer's interpretation, according to which Adrian's conversation with the devil is 'in fact only a fevered monologue'.[11] Only by shutting one's eyes to the reality of the demonic apparition of Palestrina (the city tied with an obvious pun to the *Reflections*)[12] can one maintain the 'Left critic' attitude proper to Mayer. When 'Left critics'

10 Fyodor Dostoevsky, *The Brothers Karamazov* (Richard Pevear and Larissa Volokhonsky trans) (New York: Vintage, 1992), p. 640.

11 Hans Mayer, *Thomas Mann* (Frankfurt: Suhrkamp, 1980).

12 Jesi is here connecting the town in Latium where the dialogue between Adrian and Mephistopheles takes place with Hans Pfitzner's opera Palestrina, about Giovanni Pierluigi da Palestrina, discussed by Mann in *Reflections of a Nonpolitical Man*. [Ed.]

speak of demons, they generally take them as the hallu-
cinations of the fevered. Unfortunately, this blindness or
shutting of one's eyes coincides precisely with what we
said at the beginning of the chapter—the symbols of capitalist power exercise a fascination that forces one to see
in them the *objective* and transcendent symbols of power
which today belong to the exploiters and tomorrow will
belong to the exploited.

In some occasions at least, a little Manichaeanism
would be appropriate; if nothing else, insofar as it would
force us to weigh (I am not saying to immediately accept)
what Berdyaev gleaned from Dostoevsky: 'The freedom
of man cannot be welcomed if it comes from a forced
order, as a gift from it. Human freedom must precede
such order and such harmony.'[13] What is revolt, if not the
affirmation of this principle? An affirmation that is often
distorted, altered, deliberately belittled and that yet
remains inseparable from the spirit of revolt.

In revolt, every man is engaged by his free choice.
Even if the circumstances favour the revolt—even if, as
with the Spartacist revolt, it appears as the explicit result
of a provocation—the rebel still retains that free choice
to err towards which Dostoevsky directed all of his love-
hatred.

But in the revolt every enemy is *the enemy*. Even if,
especially in modern times, the political orientation of the
organizations of the exploited has made considerable
inroads into the consciousness of the rebels (who have
nonetheless often found themselves at odds with those

13 Nikolai Berdyaev, *Dostoevsky* (Donald Attwater trans.) (Cleveland,
OH: Meridian Books, 1957).

organizations), to the point of pushing them to wrest the symbols of power from the exploiters in order to make them their own, it remains the case that the phenomenon of revolt has always determined a more or less temporary catharsis. Despite all the possible strategic concerns of the rebels, usually inspired by the traditional strategy of class organizations, in the moment of revolt the symbols of enemy power become so hostile and repugnant as to appear far more as an object to destroy than as one to appropriate. In Ivan's and Adrian's dialogues with the demon, the problem of the human interlocutor is, above all, that of the effective reality of the demonic interlocutor. But the hostility of the man towards the demon is more aristocratic disgust than violent aggression. It is not by chance that Dostoevsky explicitly alludes to the inkwell that Martin Luther threw at the Devil (Ivan throws a glass instead). It is not a genuine act of aggression; rather, it dangerously underestimates the strength of the adversary. In *Doctor Faustus*, the altered stand-in for Luther, Professor Kumpf, throws, against a non-present Devil, not even an inkwell but a breadroll. Adrian doesn't attack the demon in any way, he already belongs to him. Ivan and Adrian are in no way 'rebels'; in them, the tragedy of bourgeois civilization, born of weakness and corruption, is consummated. In the wintry and nocturnal Berlin of the Spartacists, *instead*, they fired against the demons of the city.[14] It is true, however, that to recognize in the enemy a demon, in the boss the 'monster', can elicit a singular and dangerous feeling of strength even when the military, organizational and economic

14 *Dämonen der Städte.*

balance of forces is very unfavourable. That clear-cut demonic characterization of the symbols of power of the exploiters grants a decisive value to battle but not to victory. In the nights of January 1919 in Berlin, it really seemed more important to fight the demons rather than to defeat them. Victory was already implicit in the battle.

Manichaeanism 'carries its risks'! If you don't want to give up your humanity, a battle must be won. But very few revolts have been truly victorious. We could even say that the reality of revolt is what ultimately lies behind the mythologization of defeat, the pseudo-myth of the lost battle. It is significant that in modern times, in the more recent history of class struggle, there are three episodes—the Paris Commune, the Spartacist revolt and the Spanish War—which those who today fight against capitalism would have liked to take part in. Even the October Revolution shifts to the background compared to those lost battles, probably for the very reason that it was successful (and not only because its ultimate consequences turned out to be very distant from the objectives of class struggle). A 'Manichaean' revolt (and there is no revolt that is not essentially 'Manichaean') is fated, over and above the consciousness of the rebels, not so much to vanquish the demonic adversary as to counter it with heroic victims. At its core, revolt is the most visible self-destructive form of human sacrifice. At the same time— and here human sacrifice attains its highest form—revolt is a dazzling instant of knowledge. Beyond the strategy of class organizations, the rebels recognize in a lightning-flash that the enemy is a demon or one who's sold himself to demons; the symbols of enemy power must not be incorporated but destroyed.

This then is freedom and knowledge. But its result is death, and the apologia of death—its mythologization. So it is in Johannes R. Becher's 'Hymn to Rosa Luxemburg':

> Covering you all round with verses of olive
> May a meander of tears encircle you!
> May starry nights wrap you like a mantle
> Spreading from streets of hymned scarlet blood
> [. . .]
> O thou, aroma of Elysian fields:
> You Unique You Saint! O Woman![15]

Might this not explain what the Devil says to Ivan: 'My friend, today I've adopted a special method, I'll explain it to you later'?[16]

Human sacrifices. A problem that can be summed up in a few words: 'Why is it not legitimate to kill man?' Words to which, from our vantage point, others can be added: 'Is it legitimate to get oneself killed?'

Historians have offered various interpretations and judgements about the choice of Liebknecht and Luxemburg who, in the last days of the revolt, preferred to stay in Berlin rather than find safety, though they knew that in all likelihood this meant they would be killed. It was, above all, against them that the hatred of the bourgeoisie, the Social Democrats and the military was directed; the pages of *Vorwärts* and even the posters plastered on the walls of Berlin called for their murder. Almost no one is in doubt any more that the two leaders of Spartacism could have left the capital in due time and taken refuge in some secure locality in the Reich.

15 Johannes R. Becher, 'Hymne auf Rosa Luxemburg' in *An Alle! Neue Gedichte* (Berlin: F. Pfemfert, 1919), pp. 24–6.

16 Dostoevsky, *Brothers Karamazov*, p. 640.

Arthur Rosenberg asserts that Rosa Luxemburg 'was a woman of genius, possessed of the finest intellect in the German labour movement, but there were in her remnants of a lower middle–class "decency". This is the only possible explanation for [. . .] her refusal to flee—a refusal for which she paid with her life.'[17]

A somewhat more nuanced position can be found in *Karl Liebknecht and Rosa Luxemburg* by Max Adler.[18] For Adler too, the choice that was to lead to her death was a mistake. But he adds that Luxemburg made that mistake consciously, convinced that her combative dedication— up to and including death—could contribute to repairing the weaknesses introduced into the spirit of socialism by 'social-patriotism and revolutionary fatigue'.

Clara Zetkin enriches the debate but does not speak of a 'mistake'.[19] She underscores Luxemburg's opposition to the Berlin insurrection whose failure—in light of the balance of forces—she predicted from the start; but Zetkin observes that Luxemburg felt with great intensity the duty not to abandon the masses engaged in the struggle (while considering that struggle to be tactically negative). And, since the struggle had in any case exploded, Luxemburg also felt the duty to remain to the very end side by side with her comrades, to cooperate with them in particularly critical hours.

17 Arthur Rosenberg, *A History of the German Republic* (London: Methuen, 1936), p. 85.

18 Max Adler, *Karl Liebknecht und Rosa Luxemburg* (Vienna: Verlag der Wiener Volksbuchhandlung Ig. Brand & Co., 1919).

19 Clara Zetkin, *Um Rosa Luxemburgs Stellung zur russischen Revolution* (Hamburg: Verlag der Kommunistischen Internationale, 1922), pp. 83ff.

Going even further, in *History and Class Consciousness*, Lukács notes that the guiding thread of Luxemburg's thought and of the way she lived her life was the unity of theory and praxis, 'the unity of victory and defeat and total process'.

> Theoretically she had predicted the defeat of the January rising years before it took place; tactically she foresaw it at the moment of action. Yet she remained consistently on the side of the masses and shared their fate. That is to say, the unity of theory and practice was preserved in her actions with exactly the same consistency and with exactly the same logic as that which earned her the enmity of her murderers: the opportunists of Social Democracy.[20]

To get as close as possible to Luxemburg's spiritual experience during the days of the Berlin insurrection, we should not forget how that exceptional woman, who combined 'the cheerfulness of the most cheerful child, the tenderness of the tenderest woman and the intellectual strength of the most serious man',[21] had been struggling for long, and arduously, not only against her enemies (who had caused her arrests and incarceration) but also to make her political and tactical line prevail within the Spartakusbund. The January insurrection would initially have demonstrated her scanty success in opposing the party's extremists, and finally the tragic precision of her

20 Georg Lukács, *History and Class Consciousness: Studies in Marxist Dialectics* (Rodney Livingstone trans.) (Cambridge, MA: The MIT Press, 1972), pp. 43–4.

21 Henriette Roland-Holst (Henriette van der Schalk), *Rosa Luxemburg. Ihr Leben und Wirken* (Zurich: Jean Christophe, 1937), p. 88.

forecasts. But even before January 1919, Luxemburg revealed, in a lucid and prophetic text, the weariness and strain caused by that protracted fight on multiple fronts. In November 1918, she wrote to her friends the Gecks, whose son had been killed in the final days of the war: 'We all stand under the shadow of blind fate, and it's a consolation for me that I too may perhaps soon be sent off to the other world—perhaps by a bullet from the counter-revolution that is lurking on all sides.'[22]

Luxemburg's severe and constant physical fatigue during the days of the revolt is attested by a broad range of testimonies which conversely emphasize that truly exceptional woman's extraordinary capacities to react to physical strain as well as to hand-to-hand intellectual combat. I do not wish to insist too much on this 'personal' and contingent aspect of the situation; but we should also not forget that revolt—especially a revolt undertaken in disastrous conditions, like the Spartacist one—leads, even in the physically and intellectually strongest of persons, to a concentrated expenditure of energies in the everyday impetus of a struggle that could almost be regarded as a spasmodic preparation for triumph or death.

What's more, it is unlikely that revolt will be confronted with intermediate outcomes; and, as always happens when the result of an endeavour can only be optimal or deadly, during the revolt everyone experiences at the very least the temptation of fatalism.

---

22 Rosa Luxemburg, *The Letters of Rosa Luxemburg* (Georg Adler, Peter Hudis and Annelies Laschitza eds; George Shriver trans.) (London: Verso, 2013), p. 478 (translation modified).

All these elements must be taken into consideration if we wish to confront the problem of Luxemburg and Liebknecht's ultimate choice. And one must also measure the impact—on consciousness and the unconscious—of 'historical precedents'. In his depreciation of Luxemburg and Liebknecht's sacrifice, Rosenberg writes:

> The great revolutionaries of the past realised what their persons meant in the movement. They never minded leaving their own country if it was necessary in the interests of the cause. Marx and Engels went to England in 1849 with a perfectly clear conscience, and it never occurred to them to submit themselves to the justice of the counter-revolution. Lenin left Petrograd in the summer of 1917 in order to escape persecution by the Kerensky government. He vanished into the underworld of Finland and did not return until he could reappear without danger.[23]

But a comparison with the situations of these precedents of 'strategic retreat' may, amid many other elements, have led Luxemburg and Liebknecht to behave differently. Unlike Marx and Engels in 1849 or Lenin in 1917, Luxemburg would have been forced to leave Berlin by the failure of a revolt that she did not want and which represented the opposite of her strategic line. To escape the very concrete, immediate and capital dangers of the repression would have been like evading ideological responsibility for the revolt (for which, in fact, she could

23 Rosenberg, *A History of the German Republic*, p. 85.

not hold herself responsible). But to dissociate herself from the behaviour (though she regarded it as mistaken) of the class comrades at the moment in which they faced death, and to do so after having viewed the revolt from the very beginning as ill-timed, would have meant to recognize a break between revolution and revolt. As hostile as she may have been to revolt, Luxemburg could not accept viewing it as totally other than revolution. In all likelihood, she would have never approved of our arguments about the difference between revolution and revolt, despite having been the first to predict the failure of the January revolt. She would have never rent asunder, on the basis of theoretical arguments, the connective tissue that was meant to encompass all the insurrectional movements of the exploited class, irrespective of their strategic timeliness. For her, revolution also encompassed revolt, even failed revolt. By contrast with our reflections, she placed herself on a higher plane and managed to evaluate each insurrectional phenomenon with far greater 'distance'. To justify myself—or, more to the point, to explain the reasons that lead me to advocate, in spite of it all, my point of view—I note that the aim of this text is not to formulate an ethico-historical theory of revolution, even less a historical judgement on insurrectional phenomena that have taken place up to our very day, but to contribute to the clarification of the contingent reality of some insurrectional phenomena, from yesterday and today, not without the certainty that every insurrectional phenomenon must be evaluated with a certain deliberate myopia if we really wish to experience it and use it for concrete ends.

But all this should be bracketed here. Let me sum up the nub of the question. Luxemburg could not totally dissociate revolt from revolution. She could not totally dissociate the Spartacist revolt from her person. She could not manage to be sufficiently and usefully myopic. As for Liebknecht—unlike Luxemburg, he had, at the last minute, concretely contributed to setting off the revolt. No doubt he remembered that the tortures and suicide in jail of the rector Weidig—the Hessian conspirator arrested after the distribution of the pamphlet *The Hessian Messenger*, written by Büchner and mystically retouched by Weidig—had conditioned the political vocation of his father, Wilhelm Liebknecht (a blood-relation of Weidig).[24]

We should not forget, finally, that it was precisely Luxemburg's superior ethico-political vision—which prevented her from completely dissociating revolt from revolution—that made her more susceptible to the flash of knowledge implicit in revolt. Like a spell, it placed before her—she who had been such an incisive investigator of the economic structure of capitalism—the adversary as a demonic enemy. In more banal, but also more superficial and imprecise, terms, we could say that her inability to split revolt from revolution involved her, willingly or not, in the 'psychosis of revolt'. This was all the more true for Liebknecht. The revolt could only be triumphantly won or lost in the most catastrophic manner. Were victory to come, it would not be the suppression of the enemy as much as his moral annihilation,

24 Georg Büchner, *The Hessian Messenger* (1834) in *Complete Plays: Lenz and Other Writings* (John Reddick ed. and trans.) (London: Penguin Classics, 1993), pp. 165–80.

placing a mirror before him, making him stand face-to-face with the heroic victims. The lethal spellbinding force of the capitalist symbols of power persists even when it is no longer a question of conquering those symbols—there remains, in fact, the certainty that those symbols are in some (perhaps horrid and culpable) way an 'apex', an epiphany of power; that they must be countered by an epiphany of virtue if one wishes to acquire the same power. The monster reveals itself to be the holder of *a* power when its adversaries feel the need to counter it with the power of heroic virtue (that is, with the death of the hero). And the monster has the fearsome faculty of determining the formation of its own myth, of interfering in a fundamental way in the process of the mythologization of class struggle at the precise point where revolutionary denunciation would seem to manifest itself.

We are not dealing with *sacred* tales, strictly speaking, but certainly with symbolically *true* ones which nourish propagandistic activities and make them effective because they constitute modules of knowledge and experience proper to the rebels, rooted for several generations in their psyche.

A text of incitement to revolt like *The Hessian Messenger* begins by invoking images and resorting to linguistic forms that have remained paradigmatic over decades:

> The life of the gentry is one long Sunday, they live in fine houses, wear elegant clothes, have over-fed faces and speak their own language.

And it goes on:

> [The peasant's] sweat is the salt on the gentry's table [. . .]

[T]his money is a tithe of blood squeezed from
the body of the people. [. . .]

[T]he men called by the government to maintain
order [. . .] the clothes on their back are the skin
of peasants, the spoil of the poor is in their
houses, the tears of widows and orphans are the
fat on their faces [. . .]

[C]omplain that you are subject to the whims of
a pot-bellied clique, and that these whims are
called laws [. . .]

[T]hey run their hands over thigh and shoulder
to gauge what additional burden they can bear,
and if they are merciful, then only as one spares
an ox to keep it serviceable [. . .][25]

Eighty years later, Walter Hasenclever would write:

The train derails. Twenty children croak.
Bombs kill animals and men.
No point wasting words on this.
The murderers attend *Der Rosenkavalier*.
[. . .]
They sound the drum. The noise destroys it.
Bread turns into ersatz and blood turns into beer.
My Fatherland, I'm not scared!
The murderers attend *Der Rosenkavalier*.[26]

---

25 Ibid., pp. 168–70.

26 Walter Hasenclever, 'Die Mörder sitzen im der Oper' in *Der politische
Dichter* (Berlin: E. Rowholt, 1919), pp. 25ff. Quoted in Paolo Chiarini,
*Bertolt Brecht* (Bari: Laterza, 1959). [The poem is dedicated to the mem-
ory of Karl Liebknecht.—Trans.]

Brecht, in *Saint Joan of the Stockyards* [1929–31]: Mauler, the oppressor, cries over the fate of the slaughtered calves; in *The Days of the Commune* [1978], Bismarck talks of 'extirpating with tar and sulphur', the 'damned example' of the Commune, while he strains his ear at the stage door to listen to the music of *Norma*, even singing the praises of the soprano.[27]

Borchert, in *The Man Outside* (1946): the Colonel, to the veteran who has lost everything, 'You're interrupting supper. Is it so important?'[28]

Obviously, these stories are all *true*. But truth makes them effective as expressions of revolt and materials for propaganda, because it is manifest in them in determinate stylized forms which are symbolic even at their most realistic. Recently, and by way of personal experience: in coming up with a placard for union propaganda, composed of the figure of the boss who oppresses from above the figures of the workers, it turned out to be more effective to use a drawing by George Grosz (a fat 'boss' par excellence) superimposed with the face of a well-known owner, rather than the full—and in its own way suggestive—photograph of the same boss caught at his desk in a 'sovereign' attitude. Grosz's drawing in effect confers the symbolic dimension to the propagandistic image and the superimposed photographed face determines the coincidence between symbol and everyday experience.

27 In Scene 10 of the play. Bertolt Brecht, *Saint Joan of the Stockyards* (Ralph Manheim trans.) (London: Bloomsbury, Methuen Drama, 2010). Bertolt Brecht, *The Days of the Commune* (Clive Barker and Arno Rein Frank trans) (York: Methuen, 1978).

28 Wolfgang Borchert, *The Man Outside* (Kay Boyle trans.) (New York: New Directions, 1952), p. 92.

I have deliberately mentioned literary examples that belong to German culture, certainly not because the phenomenon is solely German but because it can be studied in Germany in a particularly ample set of documents and in such a way that we can consistently match statements from properly political contexts to those from properly literary ones (even if the literature is very politicized). In particular, in the period that most interests us, namely, Germany between 1914 and Hitler's seizure of power, the mythology of class struggle took on an exceptional intensity and seemed to almost fill the 'void of values' identified by Nietzsche and his epigones. An authentic problem of values was, in fact, at stake—values that the mythological experience of class struggle conferred to everyday reality, and that later, when calmer reflection became possible, would have led Brecht to affirm his love for ordinary objects, worn because so often used—the most appropriate props in a theatre that would not be the evasion but the discussion of reality:

> [T]he pewter spoon
> Which Courage sticks
> In the lapel of her Mongolian jacket, the party card
> For warm-hearted Vlassova and the fishing net
> For the other, Spanish mother or the bronze bowl
> For dust-gathering Antigone.
> Impossible to confuse
> The split bag which the working woman carries
> For her son's leaflets, with the moneybag
> Of the keen tradeswoman. [. . .][29]

29 Bertolt Brecht, 'Weigel's Props' (John Willett trans., John Willett, Ralph Mannheim and Erich Fried eds) in *Poems, 1913–1956* (London: Methuen, 1976), p. 427.

Already in the days following the repression of the Spartacist revolt, Brecht's tone in evoking Luxemburg was rather different than that, for example, of Becher; namely, it was less 'Pindaric' than Becher's, as Paolo Chiarini underscores when he compares Becher's 'Hymn to Rosa Luxemburg' to a passage from Brecht's *Drums in the Night*.[30] This must be noted in an essay on Brecht, because it shows that Brecht's lyric was already coming into its own, with its recurrent surfacing of pathos laden with parodic or deliberately banal tonalities. But this is not our argument. The mention of Becher's 'Hymn' and *Drums in the Night* allows us, instead, to introduce the discussion of one of the most important and problematic themes in the mythology of class struggle—the agitator or rebel's sacrifice of life.

When, on 15 January 1919, Luxemburg and Liebknecht were murdered on the streets of Berlin by the men of the 'Free Corps', who embodied the Right reaction and to whom the Social Democratic government granted its complicity, the mythology of class struggle acquired among its true stories an exemplary 'precedent', in the traditional meaning of 'precedent' proper to every mythical occurrence. Photographs of political-theatre performances in Russia in 1920 show large portraits of Luxemburg and Liebknecht framing the stages on which characters carrying the symbolic markers of oppressors and oppressed acted. We can add to this some of the documents relating to the production of the 'political revue' *Despite It All* (*Trotz Alledem!*) by Felix Gasbarra, performed on 12 July 1925 in Berlin's Grosses Schauspielhaus under

30 Paolo Chiarini, *Bertolt Brecht* (Rome: Laterza, 1959).

Piscator's direction. Organized at the behest of the German Communist Party on the occasion of its party congress in Berlin, the revue was so titled in order 'to show that the social revolution continued to take place, even after the terrible disaster of 1919.' Amid the fixed and cinematographic projections, Liebknecht's body appeared in the foreground. Piscator adds however that

> The plan caused head-shaking among senior party officials at the [Central Office] meeting, because we intended to have figures like Liebknecht and Luxemburg portrayed on stage. Many felt that our plan to include members of the government in the revue (Ebert, Noske, Scheidemann, Landsberg, etc.) was dangerous. They finally consented, because no one came up with a better suggestion, but remained sceptical—all the more so since we had barely three weeks left till the day of the performance.[31]

The Goethe who with singular courage—as Mann reminds us—appended his signature to the death sentence of an infanticide knew well the meaning of human sacrifices. And *in this sense* Mann was correct to write about him 'as representative of the bourgeois age'.[32] Is *Faust* not the work of a Faustian poet? In the instant that we contrast it with the anti-Faustian *Possessed* or *Brothers Karamazov*, we realize that the notion of 'greatness' crumbles in our hands, that it is no longer possible for us to hold on to it.

31 Piscator, *The Political Theatre*, p. 92.
32 Thomas Mann, 'Goethe as Representative of the Bourgeois Age' in *Essays of Three Decades* (Helen Tracy Lowe-Porter trans.) (New York: Alfred A. Knopf, 1947).

This is really a problem of demythologization. It is a question of finding a way out of the dead end of the great sacrificers or the great victims. And to find a way out great wise men are not enough, since history teaches us how short the step is from gnosis to Manichaeanism.

# Drums in the Night

'[S]everal presumably meaningless gunshots echoed through the winter night.'[1] 'In the air, high up, a long way off, a white, wild screaming.'[2]

The first quote is from Chapter 33 of Mann's *Doctor Faustus*, the second from one of the final stage directions in Brecht's *Drums in the Night*. Both refer to the nights of the winter of 1918–19, to the revolts of Munich and Berlin. They are not casual notations and they share, besides their historical referent, the observer's detachment. The sounds of revolt are distant both from the humanist biographer of Adrian Leverkühn and from Andreas Kragler in *Drums in the Night*. In Chapter 33 of *Doctor Faustus*, devoted to the winter that followed the German defeat, and certainly not lacking in political observations, there is no overall picture, however compact, of the Munich insurrection (the city in which the protagonists are living during the revolt), or, indeed, of the one in Berlin. Only a few hurried glimpses—the meeting of 'Councils of Intellectual Workers', in which a writer 'spoke, not without charm, indeed with dimpled sybaritic fuzziness, on the topic of "Revolution and Brotherly

1 Mann, *Doctor Faustus*, p. 359.

2 Bertolt Brecht, *Drums in the Night* (John Willett trans.; John Willett and Ralph Mannheim eds) (London: Methuen, 1980), p. 53.

Love"', in front of a 'helpless, hopeless' assembly of 'buf-
foons, maniacs, specters, nasty obstructionists, and petty
daydreamers'[3]—together with some harsh reflections on
the politics of the victorious powers and of 'what little
government' Germany had, which followed their 'pater-
nal lead, joined with the National Assembly against a proletarian dictatorship, and obediently declined all Soviet
overtures, even offers to deliver grain'.[4] The revolt itself
is practically ignored; mention of it is only to be found
in the chapter's first lines, in the guise of 'revolts born of
exhaustion' (*Erschöpfungs-revolte*').[5] Its only, distant, echo
comes from 'several presumably meaningless gunshots'.[6]
Just as the shots and screams of the Spartacist revolt are
distant from Kragler in *Drums in the Night*. 'They were
the tragic figures, he the comic'—this is how Brecht
would later juxtapose the Berlin proletariat in revolt with
the 'obstreperous "hero"' of his drama.[7]

Kragler is without a doubt a comic figure, the product of the spirit of contradiction that led Brecht to subvert
the traditional expressionist picture of good men, able to
eliminate war 'by moral condemnation'.[8] And it is true
that—as Brecht himself added—this was 'a case where
revolting against a contemptible literary convention
almost amounted to contempt for a great social revolt'.[9]

3 Mann, *Doctor Faustus*, p. 359.

4 Ibid., p. 357.

5 Ibid., p. 354.

6 Ibid., p. 359.

7 Brecht, 'On Looking Through My First Plays' in *Drums in the Night*,
p. 72.

8 Ibid.

9 Ibid., p. 71.

Mann's position is far more ambiguous. The void that in Chapter 33 of *Doctor Faustus* corresponds to the 'plastic' and 'epic' reality of revolt must doubtless be blamed on the 'moderate' humanist, Serenus Zeitblom, who speaks in the first person, condemning 'bourgeois imperialism' but simultaneously experiencing 'a natural horror of radical revolution and a dictatorship of the lower classes'—though he is virtuous enough to consider the 'rule of the lower classes' as 'an ideal state in comparison [. . .] with the rule of scum'.[10] If revolt is in no way represented—meaning that, in the overall economy of the novel, it is also not deemed to be an important symbolic element—it's the fault of Zeitblom, or, in other words, it is the natural consequence of Mann's desire to show the limits and weaknesses of traditional humanism. Zeitblom sometimes says 'right things' (namely, things that Mann himself could say) but because he has to be the symbol of a tragically compromised bourgeois humanism, he cannot well and truly be 'in the right'. Let us not forget, however, that though the equation between Zeitblom and Mann is absurd, Mann himself was always very far from sharing the ideology of the rebels. One of his judgements about the communist revolt, 'an undoubtedly genuine rebellion, even if politically a mishit and historically an error',[11] could even be accepted by some Marxist historians; but it seems judicious to recognize it as the 'objective' mask of an inner repulsion—not only, as the

10 Mann, *Doctor Faustus*, pp. 357–8.

11 These words, from Mann's 'Autobiographical Sketch of My Life' are given prominent significance in Gottfried Benn's autobiography, *Double Life* (Simona Draghici trans.) (Corvallis, OR: Plutarch Press, 2002), p. 62.

writer's biography makes plain, during the days when the revolt took place but also decades later when Mann expressed himself differently than in the *Reflections of a Nonpolitical Man*.

In texts 25 years apart, both Brecht and Mann had occasion to bracket the revolt of 1918–19, and it should give us pause that this happened with two people who in other essential respects were so different. Some elements suggest that—beyond the perfectly reasonable ideological and literary explanations for the two writers' attitudes— the insurrectionary movement of winter 1918–19, and the Spartacist revolt in particular, manifested a (true or only apparent) character that could motivate that 'bracketing'.

Without a doubt the Spartacist revolt was not the work, or even the more or less distant product, of the advocates of expressionism—it was obviously not a poetic operation, if we take 'poetic operation' to mean an all-encompassing existential experience, as the theoreticians of expressionism did. The Spartacist revolt is better envisaged as a clash between classes with all the social, political, economic, psychological and military features proper to such a clash. Yet we cannot deny that it was a clash which also manifested entirely exceptional features which, while they confer upon it especially symbolic qualities, indicate a tangle of historical circumstances whose decisive impact in the history of the proletariat we must acknowledge, though we do not know whether it is repeatable. On this basis, we can say that the Spartacist revolt is paradoxically placed at the intersection between mythical time and historical time, *eternal return* and *once and for all*.

Here perhaps lies the common denominator behind the detachment from revolt in both the Brecht of *Drums in the Night* and Mann. Already in the winter of 1918–19, Brecht 'had taken sides': 'I knew next to nothing definite about the Russian revolution, but my modest experience as a medical orderly in the winter of 1918 was enough to make me think that a totally new and different permanent force had entered the arena—the revolutionary proletariat.' In the essay from which these words are taken, prefacing the 'official' edition of Brecht's theatre (Suhrkamp in West Germany, Aufbau in East Germany), the playwright notes, correctly and frankly, that in *Drums in the Night*, 'there is a faint suspicion of approval on the part of the author' for the behaviour of Kragler who 'turns his back on revolution' when he 'gets his girl back, albeit "damaged"'. Brecht chalks up his attitude at the time to his 'contradictory spirit' (towards expressionist literary conventions) which led him 'close to the limits of absurdity' as well as to the fact that his 'knowledge was not enough to make [him] realize the full seriousness of the proletarian rising in the winter of 1918–19.'[12] Even so, I think that a veritable ideological blockage lies behind these a posteriori declarations; to confirm this, it suffices to observe the contrast between the indubitable dramatic efficacy of the character of Kragler (which attains a visionary dimension in parody) and Brecht's second thoughts:

> The character of Kragler, the soldier, the petit-bourgeois, I couldn't touch. [. . .] However, I

12 Brecht, 'On Looking Through My First Plays', *Drums in the Night*, p. 72.

cautiously reinforced the other side. I gave the publican Glubb a nephew, a young worker who fell as a revolutionary during the November fighting. Though he could only be glimpsed in outline, somewhat filled in, however, thanks to the publican's scruples, this worker provided a kind of counterpart to the soldier Kragler.[13]

We may choose not to treat the following declaration by Arnolt Bronnen as entirely reliable:

Outside, the famished and freezing city twisted and turned, its buzz punctuated by the noise of the tram, betrayed by the leaders who tore each other apart in the clashes, overcome by strikes, marches, demonstrations, stock-exchange manoeuvres, rhetorical protests. In there, everything was distilled into the injections that the patient Brecht, that sharp and unflinching actor-spectator, administered to himself, with a cynicism that resembled the cut of a serrated razor: 'The *Trommeln* would really be drums, if all of this were in them,' Bronnen observed. 'Good, good, excellent,' Brecht concurred, 'I'll put it in.' 'When?' Bronnen asked. 'I already did,' Brecht replied.[14]

But even if we confine ourselves to assessing the text of *Drums in the Night* alone, we have to recognize Brecht's unmistakeable desire not only to polemicize against the 'declamatory humanitarianism' of the dramatic literature

13 Ibid., p. 73.

14 Arnolt Bronnen, *Tage mit Bertolt Brecht. Geschichte einer unvollendeten Freundshaft* (Munich: Verlag Kurt Desch, 1960), p. 28.

of the time but also to capture in the figure of Kragler the point of intersection between the atemporal dimension of the nocturnal tragedy staged on the streets of Berlin and the tragically real dimension of those events. *Eternal return* and *once and for all*—but Brecht represented that paradox not in the figure of the rebel but in that of Kragler who 'turns his back on revolution'.

But—to return to the second writer who bracketed revolt—wasn't *Doctor Faustus* too, especially in the figure of Leverkühn, the intersection between *eternal return* and *once and for all*? The events of winter 1918–19, 'which for the insightful person came not as an abrupt shock, but as the fulfilment of something long expected', 'barely elicited a shrug' from Leverkühn[15]—in whom the paradoxical synthesis of symbol and contingency, mythical time and historical time is realized. What is true is that both the young Brecht and the old Mann sensed the need to spare from the brutal domination of fate men—the rebels of that tragic winter—who had been caught up in events which, because of their twofold character as symbol and contingent history, made them into victims of a defeat that was not only military and political but also *historical* in the broadest meaning of the term, a defeat that was, above all, that of man faced with fate. The fact that the revolt of winter 1918–19 was quite clearly interpretable in this way was the common denominator between the approaches of Brecht and Mann. They offered their characters—Kragler and Leverkühn—up to fate as substitute victims of the German people, which had become the emblematic representative of humanity.

15 Mann, *Doctor Faustus*, p. 360.

Both *Drums in the Night* and *Doctor Faustus* are, in this sense, 'dramas of fate' which attempt ritually to save, by substitution and with a scapegoat, the humanity present in the German people from the defeat visited upon it by destiny. To this end, in both works, the point of intersection between *eternal return* and *once and for all* is shifted from revolt to those who 'turn their back' on it. Brecht nourished no illusions about that kind of benevolent fatefulness that for some Marxists seems to assure the victory of the proletariat, sooner or later, despite it all. He always entrusted the possibility of determining that victory exclusively to man, to his choices, to his courage, to his capacity to resist and to act appropriately. In this sense, we can say he was strongly 'Luxemburgist'. Faced with the very revolt that was least consistent with Luxemburg's thought (the revolt in which she lost her life), with its genesis and failure, which seemed to consecrate the force of fate—albeit in the opposite sense than that of 'optimistic' Marxism—Brecht reacted by creating a character, Andreas Kragler, who, in the moment he turned his back to it, was sacrificed to the revolution. What were the modalities of this sacrifice? First, making Kragler into a 'comic figure'; second, sacrificing that comic figure by infusing it with reality.

In the dead of night there's a knock at the door—it's the fiancé who's journeyed far and has returned to claim his rights over his betrothed; it's the son given up for dead coming home to his parents after a long absence; it's an unknown traveller, a god perhaps criss-crossing the earth. In the house, they're unsure whether to open the door—much menace can come from the darkness of night.

Are those hands knocking really human? Is that a human voice, asking for hospitality while remaining invisible? Even when the door is finally opened, fear and doubt persist. Is that a man standing on the threshold or a ghost? The bride-to-be recognizes her fiancé's face, the mother recovers her son's lineaments. But where does he come from? Only from terrestrial distances or from the remoteness of a kingdom of the dead?

In a song from Burgundy the mother refuses to recognize her son because she's sure she's facing a ghost; she will only allow herself to be persuaded if the man will accept to partake in her meal. In many popular German songs, adapted by the Romantics, the bride lets herself be seduced by the voice and visage of the groom-to-be and then climbs his horse which will take her to the Beyond.[16]

The figure of the returning veteran remains fundamentally ambiguous, suspended between the kingdom of the living and that of the dead—when he's a man, he's taken for a ghost; when he truly is a ghost, he's taken for one of the living. For those who stay home, those who journey far appear transfigured by *true* distance—that of death.

The evening of 30 September 1922, the audience of Munich's Kammerspiele watched the first production of a drama which evoked precisely the return of a groom-to-be. The author was Bertolt Brecht, the play *Drums in the Night*. The German artilleryman Andreas Kragler, a prisoner in Africa during the First World War and

16 On the theme of the 'return' and frequent murder of the returning veteran, see Marja Kosko, *Le fils assassiné* (Folklore Fellows Communications, no. 198) (Helsinki: Suomalainen Tiedeakatemia, 1966).

believed to be missing for four years, returns to Berlin one night in the winter of 1918–19 and discovers that, in those very hours, his fiancée Anna Balicke is entering into a new engagement with Friedrich Murk, a well-off 'draft dodger' whose child she's expecting. After a clash with her parents and Murk in Piccadilly Bar where they're celebrating the engagement, Kragler wanders all night through the streets of a Berlin turned upside down by revolution, joining groups of rebels and finally finding Anna again who has, in the meanwhile, left her parents and fiancé to come looking for him. Kragler then abandons the rebels and goes back home with Anna, pregnant with another man's child, declaring that he prefers this personal peace to battle.

Like the revenant of lore, during the first two acts Kragler appears, in the eyes of those who stayed home, as half man half ghost. In the play's first scene, in the evening, his photograph suddenly appears in an unlit room in his fiancée's parents' house. Anna's mother and father are on stage:

FRAU BALICKE *by the framed photograph of Kragler as a gunner*: He was such a good man. A man just like a child.

BALICKE: He's dead and buried by now.

FRAU BALICKE: Suppose he comes back.

BALICKE: People don't come back from heaven.

[. . .]

FRAU BALICKE: And suppose he *does* come—the corpse you say is dead and buried—back from heaven or hell? 'The name is Kragler'—who's going to tell him that he's a corpse and his girl is lying in someone else's bed?[17]

Then Anna appears. Her father wants to convince her to marry Murk:

BALICKE: [I] tell you, the fellow's dead, buried and rotten—all his bones have come apart. Four years! And not a sign of life! And his whole battery blown up! in the air! to smithereens! missing! Not so difficult to say where he's got to, eh? You're too damn scared of ghosts, that's what it is. Get yourself a man, and you won't have to be scared of ghosts any more. [. . .][18]

And here's a dialogue between Anna and Murk:

ANNA: Quiet a moment. That's a train passing in the night. Hear it? Sometimes I'm frightened he's going to turn up. I get shivers down my back.

MURK: That Egyptian mummy? Leave him to me. Here, let me tell you something—he's got to get out. No stiffs in bed between you and me. I'm not standing for another man in my bed.

ANNA: Don't get annoyed. Will you forgive me, Friedrich?

MURK: Your Saint Andrew Kragler is nothing but a ghost, can you get it into your head? He'll last as long after our wedding as after his own funeral.[19]

17 Brecht, *Drums in the Night*, p. 3.

18 Ibid., p. 5.

19 Ibid., p. 7 (translation modified).

The return of the veteran is a typical theme in expressionist theatre; the most obvious and superficial justification of its frequency lies in the desire to denounce the horrors of war which prolong themselves in the desperate condition of the returning soldier, crippled even when his body remains intact. A wide-ranging and often violent polemical debate has developed round *Drums in the Night*, which naturally coincides with the debates on the genuineness of Brecht's participation in expressionism (though it is also not easy to speak of *an* expressionism, since disparate artistic experiences and contrasting professions of faith appear to be united under that label). The recollections of Bronnen, close to Brecht at the time of the writing of the play, should be treated with a certain caution given the ambiguousness of the character, who was truly protean: first an 'expressionist' playwright (historical objectivity obliges us to put in quotation marks this now precarious qualification, much as we do with 'primitive' peoples); then, Goebbels' scrivener; finally, a polemical foe of Nazism, arrested in 1944; a friend of Austrian partisans . . . Strictly speaking, we should be interested in Bronnen's objectivity as a memorialist rather than in his political biography. But the two elements interpenetrate and condition each other, since it would be naive to trust in the serene objectivity of one who—due to personal interest or even inner disorientation—made such grave compromises. That said, and with the necessary caveats, Bronnen's testimony is of indisputable worth.

Bronnen recalls that, in the winter of 1921–22, he met Brecht for the first time in Munich at the house of Otto Zarek, that they became friends, and that, shortly thereafter, while Brecht was temporarily hospitalized in the Charité, he saw him absorbed in the writing of a *Neger-Stück*:[20] 'Bronnen interpreted this literally, imagining men with black skins, a polychromatic colouring, an exotic theme. Later it was discovered that Brecht had interpreted this misunderstanding as a sign of comprehension'.[21] This *Neger-Stück* was *Drums in the Night*. Bronnen's misapprehension immediately recalls the adjective *nègre* affixed by Rimbaud to *A Season in Hell*, and it seems legitimate to see in Brecht's satisfaction at such a 'misunderstanding' a direct reference to Rimbaud. As he remarked: 'I wrote a play (*In the Jungle of Cities*) making use of Rimbaud's heightened prose (from his *A Season in Hell*).'[22] John Willett rightly observes that, though Brecht read French poorly, Rimbaud had been translated by Theodor Däubler and Alfred Wolfenstein and was at the centre of the comedy *The Drunken Ship* (*Das trunkene Schiff*) by Paul Zech, staged around 1926 by Piscator, with sets by George Grosz. Willett insists on the reference to Rimbaud recalling the cue from *The Drunken Boat* (*Le Bateau ivre*) in *The Ship* (*Das Schiff*) and in *On the Drunken Girl* (*Vom ertrunkenen Mädchen*), integrated into *Baal*; and it would be easy to add a reference to Rimbaud's *Ophélie*.[23]

20 Black-piece or Negro-piece. [Trans.]

21 Bronnen, *Tage mit Bertolt Brecht*, p. 25.

22 Bertolt Brecht, 'On Rhymeless Verse with Irregular Rhythms' in John Willett (ed.), *Brecht on Theatre: The Development of an Aesthetic* (New York: Hill and Wang, 1977), pp. 115–20; here, p. 115.

23 Willett, *The Theatre of Bertolt Brecht*, p. 89.

*Drums in the Night* was never staged under Brecht's direction. First, because even the readers and theatre managers who appreciated Brecht the playwright were fiercely hostile to Brecht the director; then, because Brecht himself subjected his play to a negative critique; and finally, because when it was possible for him to stage what he liked he no longer thought it appropriate to stage *Drums in the Night*.

So we do not know how Brecht would have liked *Drums in the Night* to be staged when he wrote the play. We can only surmise, on the basis of some testimonies from his contemporaries, that Brecht was not at all happy with Otto Falckenberg's direction for the premiere in the Munich Kammerspiele and then for the play's reprise in the Deutsches Theater of Berlin on 20 December 1922. Bronnen remembers how Brecht was forced to accept Falckenberg so that the play could be performed but that he 'had been able perfectly to identify his weak spots (Falckenberg, in fact, isolated the characters and had no sense for more or less hidden social themes)'.[24] It also seems doubtful that Brecht approved of the rather conventional expressionist mannerism of Ludwig Sievert's stage sets: 'A flaming vision of reds and yellows, and always—above everything—the moon like a bloodshot eye. Real events in an unreal world stylised through the lyrical reality of the ballad and the dream.'

Brecht's criticism of *Drums in the Night* must have already reached negative conclusions in 1938, since the play was excluded, on the author's explicit request, from the Malik edition published that year. The terms of that

24 Bronnen, *Tage mit Bertolt Brecht*, p. 99.

criticism were then delineated by Brecht in the 1954 essay that prefaces the first volume of the Aufbau/Suhrkamp edition.

In terms of the staging of *Drums in the Night*, we can draw from Brecht's statements the following conclusions:

(a) Brecht's intent (independently of its realization) was that the play be constructed on two planes: (i) the Spartacist revolt of winter 1918–19; (ii) the bourgeois tale of Kragler, the veteran. The two planes run parallel as long as Kragler, like the rebellious proletariat, is 'the man who has suffered an unredressed wrong'. They suddenly diverge when Kragler succeeds in obtaining what had been taken away from him (his fiancée Anna) and, having got what he wanted, takes his leave from the Spartacists.

(b) The distinction between the two planes and the two stories was intended (by Brecht) to polemicize with expressionist literary convention, according to whose canons Kragler—the prototype of the *swindled man*— would not have abandoned the Spartacists, regardless of the outcome of his personal story.

(c) So the distinction and juxtaposition between the two planes and two stories had a very precise political, and not just literary, aim—to show how the revolt of the pro- letariat can be accepted as a 'romantic fact' by the bour- geois (Kragler), as long as he identifies the wrongs he's suffered in his private affairs with the wrongs suffered by the community. To show, what's more, that the authentic revolt is that of the proletariat, and that the proletariat agrees also to fight for the petty bourgeoisie while the petty bourgeoisie steps away from the battle as soon as it is no longer its personal battle.

(d) Brecht was not yet able to use the technique of the so-called 'estrangement effect': the technique, that is, which leads the spectator of the drama objectively to discuss the behaviour of the characters, rather than accepting it and making it his own as an emotional experience. Consequently, the spectator watching *Drums in the Night* can easily be led to identify with Kragler and to judge the Spartacist revolt from his point of view (the bourgeois point of view). It is especially easy for this to happen, because the spectator senses a certain sympathy for Kragler on the part of the author. In fact, however, that sympathy is dictated by the author's desire to oppose the character of the 'non-humanitarian' 'non-hero', Kragler, to the 'humanist heroes' of expressionist conventions.

The possibility of making use of these conclusions with a staging of the play in mind depends, above all, on verifying the schema proposed by Brecht with direct reference to the text.

*Act One*

In the Balicke home, the daughter, Anna, is persuaded to accept an engagement with the well-to-do Murk who is, in fact, already her lover and whose child she's expecting. The possibility of the return of her first fiancé, Kragler, missing in action, appears as a disturbing event, just like the impending Spartacist tumult. The father, Karl Balicke, says it outright:

> The masses are all worked up and without any ideals. And worst of all—I can say it here—the troops back from the front, demoralised savages, adventurers who've lost the habit of working and hold nothing sacred.[25]

Were Kragler to come back, he would probably be one of those 'demoralised savages'. Personal affairs appear to be identified with public ones. Towards the end of the act, the journalist Babusch brings news of the imminent Spartacist revolt. And shortly before the end, almost to confirm the proximate danger of subversion, both public and private, Kragler appears, back from his African captivity. In the text, he voices his first lines not as 'Kragler' but as 'The Man':

THE MAN: The name is Kragler.[26]

This is not just the return of the fiancé taken for dead but the appearance of a symbol—'The Man'—in which the Balicke family recognizes the menacing Spartacus. This is the moment of greatest identity between the two planes (that of revolution and that of Kragler's private story). If we didn't know the play's ending, we could see in the identification of Kragler with 'The Man' a commonplace of expressionist convention—the suffering or swindled man has no name, he is 'The Man'.

*Act Two*

In Piccadilly Bar, Kragler argues with Anna's parents and Murk. His disturbing presence is directly equated with that of the Spartacists in the streets:

BALICKE *sobered up somewhat, hurries in*: Sit down. (*He draws the curtain, there is a metallic sound.*) He's got the red moon with him and rifles behind him in Babusch's newspaper district.[27]

---

25 Brecht, *Drums in the Night*, p. 9 (translation modified).

26 Ibid., p. 13.

27 Ibid., p. 22 (translation modified).

In the discussion between Kragler, Anna and the others, the sufferings undergone by Kragler and the wrong done to him by the one who's stolen his fiancée are denounced in the hallucinated tone of the great expressionist 'laments'. Kragler's drama seems to be evoked in terms of a desperate human condition. There is still a relationship with historical circumstances but the painful consequences of history are envisaged in an apocalyptic language drawn more from personal drama than collective tragedy.

The differentiation between the two planes (the revolution and Kragler's story) is underscored in the closing exchanges in which Kragler's fate is explicitly contrasted (and downplayed as a 'private sentimental matter') with the revolt of the Spartacists:

> *Silence. In the next room The Man can be heard asking 'What's happening?' The waiter answers him, talking through the door left.*
>
> WAITER: The crocodile-hide suitor from Africa has been waiting for four years and the bride still has her lily in her hand. But the other suitor, a man with buttoned boots, won't give her up and the bride who still has her lily in her hand doesn't know which side to go off.
>
> VOICE: Anything else?
>
> WAITER: The revolution in the newspaper district also has a certain significance and then the bride has a secret, something the suitor from Africa who has been waiting for four years doesn't know about. It's still quite undecided.
>
> VOICE: No decision one way or the other?

WAITER: It's still quite undecided.[28]

The line 'The revolution in the newspaper district also has *a certain significance*' reveals the fault line between the two planes.

*Act Three*

Kragler and Anna wander separately through the night, confronted with the horizon of revolt. Anna looks for Kragler. The identification between the two planes and the doubt cast upon it are particularly explicit in the dialogue between the journalist Babusch and the waiter Manke:

> MANKE: My affair? The stars run clean off their rails if a man's left unmoved by unfairness. (*Seizes his own throat.*) It's driving me too. It's got me by the throat too. A man on the cross is nothing to be petty about.
>
> BABUSCH: What cross or no cross? [. . .] I'm telling you, something's going to be bellowing like a bull down at the newspapers before daybreak. And that'll be the mob thinking there's a chance to settle old scores.[29]

In Babusch's words is a patent refusal of the humanist rhetoric of expressionism—it's not about the man 'on the cross', *that determinate man on the cross*; it's not about a particular injustice. A great revolt is at stake. But Babusch is the reactionary journalist. It is significant that Brecht gave him the function of spokesman of the revolt with the obvious aim of objectivating it.

28 Ibid., pp. 30–1.
29 Ibid., pp. 35–6.

The transformation of Kragler's drama into 'comedy' (as Brecht puts it) is also evident at those points where his participation in the revolt is understood as a sentimental melodrama:

> MANKE: And he is swallowed up by the newspaper district. Awaited by the schnapps saloons. The night! The misery! The dregs! Rescue him!
>
> BABUSCH: All this is a drama called *The Angel of the Dockland Boozers*.[30]

With clear parodic intent, Kragler's drama is evoked shortly thereafter:

> MANKE: The lover has already vanished, but his beloved hastens after him on wings of love. The hero has been brought low, but his path to heaven is already prepared.[31]

And at the end of the act the same character '*Spreads both his arms widely once more*':

> The revolution is swallowing them up. Will they find each other?

*Act Four*

The distinction between the two planes is stressed in the exchanges between Kragler and the publican Glubb. Kragler, drunk, is 'the one who has suffered a wrong' but he is also 'the one who has lost hope in the results of the revolution':

> KRAGLER: Therefore make yourselves at home on our planet, it's cold here and rather dark, Red,

30 Ibid., p. 36.
31 Ibid., p. 37.

the world's too old for the millennium and
heaven has been let, my friends.[32]

Like Brecht pointed out in his a posteriori critique,
the figure of Glubb's nephew, a young worker killed
during the November days, tends to contrast with that of
Kragler—Kragler is the bourgeois caught up in the revolution by the wrongs he's personally suffered and no
more; Glubb's nephew is the proletarian who dies during
the revolution, fighting for himself and for everyone.

At the beginning of the act, Glubb sings the ballad
of the dead soldier which no doubt also frames Kragler's
predicament in the general context of the times. But Kragler's personal conduct tends to separate the returning
veteran from the proletarians in revolt.

*Act Five*

Having set off with the other Spartacists towards the
newspaper quarter in which the fighting is taking place,
Kragler runs into Anna and ends up abandoning the
rebels in order to return home with her. Voices 'of record'
announce that the revolution risks failing:

THE ONE: We're far too few.

THE OTHER: Far more are on the way.

THE ONE: Far too late.[33]

The definitive split between the two planes is consummated with Kragler's abandonment of the Spartacists;
he regains his fiancée—even though she was made pregnant by someone else—and prefers to leave with her
rather than 'plunge into the vortex' of the revolution.

32 Ibid., p. 44.
33 Ibid., p. 48.

The 'romantic' image of the revolution to which Kragler had initially rallied is transformed into a tragic theatrical *mise en scène*:

> KRAGLER: I'm fed up to here. (*He laughs irritably.*)
> It's just play-acting. Boards and a paper moon and the butchery off-stage, which is the only real part of it.[34]

Kragler has lost all hope in the revolution. He recognizes the massacre of the revolutionaries to be as tragically fated as the wrongs he himself has suffered and, now that he can at least regain the woman, abandons the Spartacists and the revolt.

Almost a century has passed from when Nietzsche's demon or fate saw to it to remove from the 20 or so volumes planned for *Ancient Reflections* (*Altertümliche Betrachtungen*), the only fragment that should have survived. The weight of that choice, which dramatically opposed *The Birth of Tragedy* to Schiller's *On Naïve and Sentimental Poetry*, possesses the genuine value of an epiphany, conserving inviolate the doubleness of a suddenly manifested deity. It was not, in fact, a question of *God* who struck high on Nietzsche's soul, not revealing His countenance, but of *a God*, Dionysus, ready to grant name and image to those wishing to contemplate him. But the named and observed god was also God, the unknown one, and while He disclosed Himself to His solitary devotee He obliged him to serve Him; similarly, in the *Parsifal*, Kundry would have identified 'service' as the sole consequence of the contemplated epiphany.

---

34 Ibid., p. 52.

'I want to know you and serve you!'—this is how Nietzsche addressed himself to the unknown God, acknowledging His paradox while losing himself in the epiphany; and yet he welcomed epiphanic images (the name and the face), placing himself before their divine source almost as though in a relationship of power to power.

What really matters about the past is what we cannot remember. The rest, what memory conserves or retrieves, is mere sediment. A part of time passed has really become part, like a digested nutrient, of the living organism; it continues to be *past* but it is the only true living past and it lives in the brain and the blood, ignored by memory. The traditional saying 'Far from the eyes, far from the heart' can be paradoxically inverted. If in a bygone time a face inspired authentic love or authentic hate (or respect or contempt), the remembering of the lineaments of that face may remain or return with clarity and precision in memory but it will be *past*—in the sense of a dead, imprisoning past—while the genuine experience of love or hate will not be remembered; only its circumstances and semblance will be, and it will endure, alive.

To represent, *to repeat*, is a gesture that cannot be genuinely carried out unless one takes into account the profound contrast, or better yet the radical opposition, between remembrance and survival, memory and duration. To represent *Drums in the Night* does not mean giving life back to the memory of what Brecht experienced. Above all, it means letting that part of the past which cannot be remembered, and which is constituted by the drama, live within oneself. This ritualization of theatrical experience is placed on the same plane as the 'representativeness' of revolt. Revolt, as I have said, tends to be the intersection between the *eternal return* and the *once and for all*. In this regard, the Spartacist revolt is especially emblematic. The inner dialectic between individual time and collective time externalizes itself in moment of battle as does the dialectic between the conduct of an ideological group and the history of a nation, or, indeed, the history of Europe.

But in the externalization of that dialectic, symbols and myths come to reveal the precedents and conditionings determined by a 'once upon a time' which takes on divine or demonic features and against which the revolt acts. In this singular dimension, the Kragler of *Drums in the Night* is sacrificed to the fate of the German people, just as in Storm's *Immensee*, Reinhard, who gives up Elisabeth, is sacrificed to the moral norm of the bourgeoisie in its last moment of greatness. And it is the same existential sacrifice that manifests itself as turning one's back on the revolt in one case and as renouncing a woman in the other. Both are, paradoxically, moments of revolt, hours of an uninterrupted battle.

Storm finished a first version of *Immensee* in 1850. This date must be considered in two separate contexts, in the flow of two seemingly different stories, each of which is identified with a different experience of time. One is the personal story of Theodor Storm, which takes its inner and solitary rhythm from the writer's life; the other is the story of Europe, the history of European spirit— the abstraction, if you will, or the transcendental synthesis of the existential conditions of those who lived through those years. The images of each, their apparent impetus, seem to lead us beyond their mutable semblances to a static nucleus, the essence or epiphany of the realities that were present within them. Despite this reference to the origins, to dark roots or destinies, the two stories also bear witness to two different experiences of transitoriness, understood as a dimension that is simultaneously spatial and temporal and within which the individual man and the men of his time meet and communicate, drawing a provisional individuality—he and 'the others'—from their reciprocal relationship. The one is not less true, within such dimensions, than the 'others', and this reality is dialectically opposed to the (immobile) reality in which the one and the 'others' are individual and intimately solitary shards of truth.

When Storm wrote *Immensee*, nine years had passed since giving up Berta von Buchau, the 'historical' counterpart to the Elisabeth of the novel. It had been four years since Storm's marriage to his cousin Costanze Esmarch, to whom the second and definitive version of *Immensee* was to be dedicated. But, already in the first years of the marriage, a new epiphany of the eternal feminine image had found its way into Storm's life, an epiphany to which he was destined to submit and which he would eventually hallow after long spiritual sufferings and hesitations. Doris Iensen—whom fate would have tragically allowed to become Storm's second wife—had appeared to him, bearing a new and problematic seductive force. More than 20 years after *Immensee*, the novella *Viola Tricolor* once again places the drama of the multiple epiphanies of Aphrodite at the heart of bourgeois morality; in both novellas, the cruelty of renunciation or, inversely, of the substitution of love, is cured by an act of devotion to the continuity of life, lived in solemn respect for bourgeois morality. The renunciation of a love that has become illicit or the overcoming of the exclusive aspects of the love for a dead spouse are delineated in their rigorously juridical character—in both cases, the protagonists of the novellas behave in accordance with the dictates of the extant law of their community. Yet in both cases, symbols that transcend the rationality of legal institutions—the unattainable water lily or access to the secret garden—accord a supreme, metaphysical charisma to the conduct which is in harmony with those institutions, so that the law of men comes to be identified with the dark norm of being and licit behaviour becomes an act of devotion. The first version of *Immensee* contains the description of Reinhard's life after his separation from Elisabeth (his wedding, his tranquil existence, which doesn't efface how much he misses his beloved from the time of the *Jugendzauber*, the youthful enchantment). In the definitive version, the novella encloses the object and moment of renunciation within the solitary fate of an old man who knows shadows and light to the point that he can shepherd presences round himself to evocative effect; it is dedicated to Costanze.

1850: Goethe has been dead for 18 years; in Berlin, Storm makes the acquaintance of Joseph Freiherr von Eichendorff and Theodor Fontane. A secret and subterranean bond links *Immensee* to *Werther*, looking backwards, and to *Taugenicht*[35] and *Effi Briest*,[36] looking forwards.

---

35 *Aus dem Leben eines Taugenichts* (Life of a Good-For-Nothing), a novella from 1826 by Joseph Freiherr von Eichendorff.

36 A novel by Theodor Fontane, published in 1896.

The old tale of the pretenders who vie for the princess' hand—drawing on the historical substrate of primordial social institutions—has survived in the psyche of modern man not so much as the actual competition between champions who fight one another with the weapons that each has been accorded by fate but as the site of the epiphany of a mysterious contender who has arrived on the testing ground with weapons draped in darkness. It is futile to ask him to lift his cloak and reveal his face when his victory is already certain; for it is in victory itself that the mysterious contender seems to plunge deeper into the shadows, dragging the conquered bride with him into that darkness.

In the span of time between 1774 and 1862, between the publication of Goethe's *Werther* and Fromentin's *Dominique*,[37] the masked knight appears repeatedly, in guises whose mediocrity betrays the hostility of a narrator who has entered into battle against the mysterious antagonist. Neither Albrecht, Lotte's groom, nor the Count of Nièvres, who snatches Madeleine from Dominique, nor, finally, in *Immensee*, Erich, the friend 'who looks like his greatcoat' and marries Elisabeth, rendering her inaccessible to Reinhard, possess the dark and noble lineaments of that ancient black knight. In all three stories, the drama of the thwarted pretender is depicted in a bourgeois frame and, what's more, the lucky winner lacks any apparent extraordinariness—he is a man like all others, inferior, at least in certain aspects, to the pretender with whom the narrator sides, and yet favoured by circumstances and fate. The dark knight thus becomes ever

37 A novel by Eugène Fromentin, first published in 1862.

more mysterious and his mystery becomes the existential mystery of man's destiny because the ancient symbol is no longer such and it would be reduced to allegory were it to be conserved in its bygone forms. Only with Kafka, and *The Castle* in particular, will the antagonist return to being a symbol—a symbol closed in on itself.

If, as we have said, the stories of contests for the princess' hand sink their roots in primordial nuptial institutions, the mysterious and victorious antagonist, the black knight, is a late but not too faded reflection of the extra-human presence—it would not be entirely exact to call it 'divine'—which intervenes with its fearsome epiphany at the moment of matrimony and interposes itself between the spouses on their wedding night. The mythical and sacred reality of the sexual experience encompassed within the sphere of matrimony could be grounded and essentially resolved through the ritual deflowering of the virgin by an extra-human entity which (in different ways) would thereby establish the precedent required for the sacred foundation of intercourse and eliminate the dangers harboured by an adventure into the unknown territory of the sacred devoid of tutelary precedents.

From *Werther* to *Immensee* and *Dominique*, the inescapable presence of that entity becomes nothing more than an ingredient of tragedy, having been displaced from the ordered sphere of the sacred to that of fate and marked by an order which, in each of its parts, is inaccessible to ritual. In fact, a ritual has survived, from the time of ancient contests for the conquest of the bride, but it is a purely negative ritual; a morality, in other words, the one that must be respected for a man to be a man and whose only name is renunciation.

While it thereby becomes ever darker, the face of the mysterious knight, the lucky contender who conquers the bride, actually reveals its name at the very moment that it consigns that name to a dark abyss. That name is Death. Beyond the semblances of the *eternal triangle*—which literature has by now made threadbare—Werther, Reinhard or Dominique have death as their antagonist; it is death that takes their bride from them, just as in Romantic ballads it is the dead knight who knocks at the door of his betrothed and drags her on his horse to the Beyond.

In a time when 'even the Chinese' paint Lotte and Werther on glass,[38] no one should have any doubts about the call of death harboured by Werther's love for Lotte. In Werther's story, death comes precisely because love cannot attain completion—it encounters a moral obstacle that is transfigured in the image of Albrecht as well as in the moral law, in the guise of the unknown knight.

In reality, Lotte Buff and Goethe did not die. Who did die, at 28 years of age, was Jenny Chessé, the young Creole woman buried in the cemetery of Saint-Maurice and to whom the schoolboy Fromentin irrevocably tied his life—the Madeleine of *Dominique*. An explicit presage of death can already be found in Madeleine's goodbye to Dominique in that castle of Nièvres where the air is unhealthy and the ailing are abandoned. The Count of Nièvres, the lucky contender, the kidnapper, is far away, having led the bride into the kingdom of death and

---

38 Jesi is referencing Goethe's *Venetian Epigrams* [1790], XXXIVb: 'The Chinese paints, with trembling hand, Werther and Lotte on glass.' [Trans.]

beyond reprieve. Some piercing observations by Dominique, such as Madeleine's hair brushing against his lips during the evening at the theatre-box, make it clear that the force of the unknown knight has become moral law, the sovereignty of death over the experiences of man; and Madeleine's horror after her abandonment, which comes before the final leave-taking from Dominique, is the reaction of a dead woman who returns to her condition after having been called back to life for an instant.

There is a famous novella by Hans Christian Andersen entitled *The Old House* (*Det Gamle Huus*). We do not know to what extent the Danish writer thought of *Immensee* as he composed it but it is certain that some of Storm's dominant images return here, altered and faded. What we are interested in is not a problem of literary derivations or influences; we will, instead, attend to the initially imperceptible change in faces and object which hides a deep metamorphosis of the spirit. In Andersen's novella, an old house and an old man endure as survivals of the time spent among buildings and people pregnant with youth. The old man lives alone, all his friends having died years ago, and he continues to wear the now unfashionable outfits of his youth; the old house conserves, within and without itself, the symbols and furnishings of the past; it is itself a decaying relic. Among those testimonies of bygone days there stands out the portrait of a young woman, she too long dead; the bouquet of wilted flowers in a vase modestly alludes to the old man's past love.

It seems we find ourselves at the beginning of *Immensee*—an old man, in outdated clothes, in an old house, before the portrait of a woman who now belongs only to the past. In fact, beyond the initial analogy, many things differ. Andersen's old man is a faded and pathetic wraith whose solitude the young generations want to assuage, almost out of pity. The old house has become almost grotesque in its forms, decorations and furnishings; it is not devoid of charm but that charm is ambiguous, far from life; it is the charm of old cellars and old attics, of derelict castles and bizarre ruins. Even if the child of the young family immediately strikes a bond of sympathy with the old house and the old man, any continuity between the lives of the two generations is absent; and when that child will have become an adult, he will go to live in a new building, built at the cost of the old house's demolition.

The severe pathos of *Immensee*'s first lines is replaced in Andersen's tale by a moderate humour, intended to remedy the fear of death. Impending death hangs over the old man who has merely been granted a brief earthly parenthesis; and the old house is 'a family grave':

> All the other houses in the street were very new and neat, with large window-panes and smooth walls. You could see, well enough, that they didn't want to have anything to do with the old house. You could see they were thinking: 'How long is this old rubbish-heap going to stand there, making an exhibition of itself, in our street? [. . .] The iron railings look like the gate on an old family grave.'[39]

39 Hans Christian Andersen, 'The Old House' in *Hans Andersen Forty-Two Stories* (Montague Rhodes James trans.) (London: Faber and Faber, 1953) (translation modified).

The house in which *Immensee* begins, the house of the old Reinhard, is also ultimately a grave. But the experience of death for the protagonist of Storm's novella is far deeper and more mysterious, far more intimately tied to life, than what we can glimpse from Andersen's funereal hints. In *Immensee* there lives the spirit of tragedy— of death lived day-to-day. The old Reinhard too has become almost 'a stranger', like the old man; but his gaze is 'piercing' and his black eyes are 'still lustrous with the fire of lost youth'.

Rather than limiting himself to keeping the pathetic dried flowers under the portrait of his beloved, Reinhard undertakes a mysterious invocatory ritual. 'No light yet!' he orders the old governess. Then he sits in the shadows of a room that had until then been locked and waits, with joined hands. 'As the dark gradually came on, a ray of moonlight streamed through the window panes, bathing the paintings hung on the wall.' It seems that Reinhard does not know what will happen: 'As it crept slowly along the wall, the old man's gaze *involuntarily* followed.' Then, the mystery or miracle: 'At last it reached a little portrait in a simple black frame and irradiated the face. He rose and went to the picture. "Elisabeth!" the old man murmured. At the sound of that name, time was transformed—he was a youth again.'[40]

The return of time past could find a solemn paradigm in the dedication to *Faust*; already in those verses, Goethe, with the assuredness that comes with old age, had come closer to the mystery of the invocatory act which requires the participation of will but does not lose its fatefulness,

40 Storm, *Immensee*.

like a mythical epiphany. When Reinhard refuses the light and waits in the shadows of dusk, he doesn't know what will happen; yet a force that coincides with his will compels him to the ritual acts that precede invocation—darkness and solitude. A ray of moonlight comes but the present also turns into the past because there echoes the name: 'Elisabeth!' Will and fate can no longer be kept apart. Here lies the entire meaning of *Immensee*—will and fate, renunciation and fateful loss partake in the same reality; they are the face of the real, one and indivisible.

What does it mean to renounce? Renouncing is a gesture and as such—as Kierkegaard would say—it is the reality in which form lives, in which life is true and absolute. But that means that there opens up, before the one who renounces, the labyrinth of being. This is because only those who execute a gesture are destined to confront the illuminations and terrors of the epiphanies of the true. It is not solely a matter of lightning strikes and dark shadows. In the very instant in which life appears to be true, the infinite wefts of the possible—and thus of the not-true—reveal themselves to the observer, and truth, exact vision, lies behind him. He has chosen and attained truth; but that is why truth now lies behind him, like a natal abyss, and before him lies nothingness, darkness. 'Before him outstretched the great wide world'. The hour when Reinhard, at the end of *Immensee*, renounces Elisabeth for ever, is that of dawn: 'The world outside was flooded with the glory of morning light.'[41]

41 Ibid.

But beyond the page that closes the penultimate chapter of *Immensee*, darkness returns: 'The moon shone no longer through the window panes. The room grew dark.' Thence is born the flower of darkness, the unreachable flower of death:

> But the old man sat yet a while with folded arms in his armchair, lost in revery. Gradually the darkness all about him changed to a great dark lake. A black, mysterious body of water stretched far into the distance, ever darker, ever deeper, ever more mysterious, and at last, so far away that the old man's eyes could hardly discern it, he saw a white water lily floating in solitary beauty and purity.[42]

There is no explanation for all of this, and there must not be. Since renunciation is a gesture, lifting the eyelid before the epiphany of the true, it is closed in on itself, repelling every explanation as well as every paraphrase. In this sense, the ending of *Immensee* is identical to the ending of *Werther*. A singular symmetry links the two conclusions, that of the continuity of life: 'He drew up his chair to the table, took one of the open books, and buried himself in the studies which were his passionate delight in his lost youth'; the break of death: 'Guildsmen bore his body. No priest attended him.'[43] The same character, the one who has given up, stands between two mirrors which varyingly reflect his face and pass these images between each other. The one who abides between the two mirrors

42 Ibid.

43 Johann Wolfgang Goethe, *The Sorrows of Young Werther* (Michael Hulse trans.) (London: Penguin, 1989), p. 134.

has carried out his renunciation—he is dead among the living and living among the dead. Neither life nor death possess him entirely because he has chosen and carried out the gesture, transforming his life into a truth which can only be extraneous to life and death because neither life nor death can contain it univocally. Moreover, this means that he will always be a stranger, foreign, in the face of life and death. Werther's painful agony and his tawdry funeral bear witness to how difficult it was for him to die, he who had known truth in renunciation. Similarly, Reinhard's foreignness among his fellow citizens ('apparently he was a stranger') betrays an analogous difficulty in living, a detachment with regard to those who live while thinking themselves familiar with life. But Werther seemed to have made renunciation coincide with death, while for Reinhard it equated with survival. One with the mask of the dead, the other with the mask of the living, both welcomed the epiphany of the true.

Written 80 years after *Werther*, *Immensee* could be understood as an answer to the same question about the nature of renunciation and its moral value. If *Werther* is truly a painstakingly attentive analysis and ultimately a denunciation of sentimental self-delusions and of the narcissistic introspection from which they spring, and if *Immensee* (in keeping with Lukács's interpretation of Storm's art and ethics) is proof, in the severe vocation of the last great bourgeois artist, of the equation between the duty-bound gesture and life's sole reality, then it becomes legitimate to identify a continuous line stretching between the two works—a line that proceeds from the overcoming of pietist morality, always bordering on pathos, in the name of bourgeois morality; achieving the late, and perhaps epic epiphany of that very same morality. If we were to accept this picture, then we should fully agree with Mann when in one of his essays he spoke of Goethe as a 'representative of the bourgeois age'.

There is also another line, deep and secret, linking *Werther* to *Immensee*. About it we can say, to begin with, that it is founded on the shared will (or need) in both cases to invoke an amorous drama—the particular drama that stems from a love that ends with renunciation. The fated nature of both renunciations transposes the two amorous dramas from the particular to the universal, or, at least, to the universally human, turning them almost into the paradigm of a determinate erotic relationship—the first love, the love of one's youth (even if tragedy is here masked by the seeming banality of the circumstances: Lotte already engaged, Elisabeth reluctantly pushed by her mother into a marriage with Erich). When he wrote *Werther*, Goethe was only 25 and so not very far, in terms of objective chronology, from the events of his life evoked in the novel. But the application of 'objective' chronology to the history of spirit is precarious, and pining for lost youth is often tragically genuine among those who 'objectively' have yet to leave it behind. *Immensee* is the work of a 32-year-old man, himself not so distant from the narrated events. Yet the 32-year-old Storm does not hesitate to embody himself in the 'old man' who, through a mysterious invocation, retrieves time passed. The yearning for youth in *Werther* is already made evident enough by the celebration of the great, panic spring with which the novel opens. It finds pathetic confirmation in the affectionate care with which Goethe, without reneging his final verdict, follows the stirrings of Werther's soul—they may be self-delusions but they remain experiences of an unrepeatable hour, alive with mysterious abandonments, even if devoid of wisdom. Likewise, in *Immensee*, the memories of youth are missed so strongly as to merge with the invocation of that time which, through secret bonds, man yearns for above all—childhood.

Turning yearningly towards one's youth when it is gone fundamentally means allowing oneself to be ruled by the desire or certainty of immortality. But immortality in this sense does not mean the absence of the death that exists beside life, within life and after life—it means refusing to die, refusing the instant and the event that apparently conclude life, or even open onto another one.

Is *Werther*—in particular, Werther's death, his awful agony and squalid funeral—really a resolute condemnation of self-delusions? Does it not instead communicate the difficulty that Werther has in dying, his intimate foreignness to the gesture that gives death? On what he will be after death, Goethe remains silent (this would seem to vindicate Ladislao Mittner when he argues that the narration of that death is 'the refutation, on the artistic plane, of Werther's hasty and amateurish faith in immortality');[44] but Goethe insists on Werther's difficulties in dying—more than 12 hours of agony with a crushed skull. For Werther, however, living is equally difficult.

44 Ladislao Mittner, 'Il "Werther", romanzo antiwertheriano' in *La letteratura tedesca del Novecento. Con tre saggi su Goethe* (Turin: Einaudi, 1960), p. 88.

After the first letters—the second in particular—in which Werther opens his entire soul to the epiphany of nature in spring, he seems to be readying himself to becoming ever more a stranger from the living and the earth; the recurrent mentions of suicide and even the reading of Ossian are so many stages in this preparation. The moment in which the fruits of that preparation will mature is the hour of renunciation, the decision of suicide. But the difficulty in attaining death shows that taking one's distance from life is not an authentic preparation for dying. Werther on the threshold of the Beyond is a stranger to the living, but he is also a stranger to dying. This does not mean that he has become a stranger to life and death, since life and death are not exhausted in the act of living or dying, nor (which amounts to the same) does man realize his whole self in living or in dying.

There is one reality, however, that Werther, in the final hours of his life, is not a stranger to—the reality of renunciation. 'Lotte, farewell!'—in his last cry, Werther is truly himself; in the hour of renunciation, his being is true. If his preceding vicissitudes, including his love for Lotte, appear marked by self-delusion, show Werther to be, in Kierkegaardian terms, an 'inauthentic' man, renunciation grants, for the first time, authenticity to his being and truth to his life.

But the authentic experience of life, the experience that transforms existence, with its infinite possibilities, into reality, estranges one from those unreal infinite possibilities, because it encloses being in the gesture; and Werther's true gesture is renunciation—not suicide. This looks like a paradox. And yet what Werther really wants is a gesture that would make true, make real, his relationship with Lotte—renunciation. But, it will be objected, in order to carry out this renunciation he resorts to suicide. But renunciation and suicide cannot be equated. Werther chooses renunciation, and feels himself such a stranger from existence, so abandoned by existence, as to slip into suicide. In the novel, suicide follows quick on the heels of renunciation, and, from the very first moment in which Werther thinks of renunciation, he does not dissociate it from suicide. The simultaneity between the thinking of the gesture and its consequence is fateful, but it is not an identity. And, in fact, while for Werther it will prove 'easy' to renounce, it will instead prove 'difficult' to die.

One would need to dig deep into Goethe's mind to discern why Werther would have wanted, as a consequence of his renunciation, a 'difficult' suicide instead of a 'difficult' survival. Goethe committed to paper that he had himself been on the verge of suicide, testing whether he had the courage to stick a dagger in his chest. The courage wasn't there and no suicide took place. But Goethe was cruel with his character, destining him to death, even though he allowed him the relative advantage of the pistol over the dagger. It's the mysterious exchange of author and character; but this is a ritual—not a liberation. It is hollow to speak of liberation and catharsis when it comes to Goethe, who didn't take his own life because he had Werther die a suicide. Goethe was well aware that there is no liberation, no liberating reality, without the gesture. But he was equally conscious of the value of ritual and he carried out the ritual of human sacrifice on Werther—a ritual that is not the liberation from latent forces but exorcism or consecration. He was later to carry out an analogous sacrifice with Eduard and Ottilie in *Elective Affinities*.[45] Both novels are above all ritual acts that require victims. Because the gesture of the character is not the gesture of the author, the art of the writer allows no liberation. Yet in its eminently magical reality it permits the ritual, exorcism, consecration. The word is the primary element of ritual and it can replace any cultic ornament; the indispensable gesture is carried out because the author wields the word like a sacrificial knife. Gretchen in *Faust* is also, or especially, a ritual victim. Over and above the most immediate moral interpretation of her death, the latter lets her attain a sphere of myth where she takes on the features of the infernal *kore* (the scene of the Walpurgis Night); with her death, she guarantees the deliverance of Faust's soul, just as once upon a time the Kore of Eleusis granted passage to the Beyond. But in *Faust*, the dead Gretchen is identified with the gorgon—the primordial, healing myth is lost, and the redemptive image of the *kore* is now accompanied by the horrors of the hereafter, the menace of death. Yet that menace is not death but dying—Werther's 'difficult' suicide. Goethe's greatness here consists in having proved that even that fatal alteration of myth can damage only the semblances of being—such as Werther's act of dying—but not death.

Werther does not violate the virgin but renounces her and is therefore destined to encounter the gorgon in the act that gives death. Faust violates the virgin because

45 Johann Wolfgang von Goethe, *Elective Affinities* (R. J. Hollingdale trans. and introd.) (London: Penguin Classics, 1971).

the ritual he follows is overseen by the demon; and the demon will offer the living Faust the horrid vision of a beheaded Medusa. In *Faust*, but not in *Werther*, the demon is named and present—in a way, Goethe is more sincere, or perhaps his gaze is keener and more resolute. Thanks to this, Faust will contemplate the horror of the gorgon while still alive while Werther will only experience it on the threshold of death.

Faust does not give up. How ambiguous is the figure of Goethe as 'representative of the bourgeois age'! Faust does not give up—he welcomes the demon, and notwithstanding this he will have deliverance. Werther gives up. He is not granted knowledge of the true face of the demon. In the gesture of wanting death, Werther is subjected to the face of the gorgon; afterwards, we know nothing more about him.

The plurality of Goethe's spirit allows us to see in *Faust* a veritable parallel universe to that of the other works. While *Werther*, and later *Elective Affinities*, are the symbols of the gesture that makes being true in the instant in which it estranges it from life and death, *Faust* is the song of abandonment and fate—the song of the grace that rules over the semblances of being and redeems. It might already seem ambiguous to group *Werther* and *Elective Affinities*, since the choice of the gesture stands out starkly in the first novel, while in the second the gesture is guided by a cosmic fate, almost leading it to grace. But in *Elective Affinities* too there persists the gesture that consecrates existence, making it true, even though it also opens the way to horror. In *Faust*, the gesture is absent, action is abandonment, life is a fate that cannot be consecrated—alone and sovereign stands grace.

So what is the gesture? Only the product of the unknown and unspoken presence of the demon. When the demon appears, the gesture dissipates—it was the demon's mask—and man lives abandoned in the 'dark gallery', where the heights are equal to the depths in which the god will appear.

# The Untimeliness of Revolt

In the famous opening lines of Chapter 8 of *Beyond Good and Evil*, devoted to the prelude of the *Master-Singers*, Nietzsche writes: 'This kind of music best expresses what I consider true of the Germans: they are of the day before yesterday and the day after tomorrow—*they have as yet no today*.'[1] It was this assertion that I had in mind when I placed the Spartacist revolt at the crossroads between the once and for all and the eternal return—not so much of historical time and mythical time (according to the dialectic favoured by Mircea Eliade) but of the day before yesterday and the day after tomorrow. A similar placement can be explained at various levels, each of which does not exclude the others. To begin with, we can say (remaining very close to the surface) that precedents and forces from the past exerted their pressure and manifested themselves in the Berlin insurrection, so that it did not only spring from the contradictions of the time preceding it but also harboured within itself ponderous elements of that past, elements that could only be exorcised by a 'day after tomorrow' capable of grinding down the survivals of the past, greatly diminishing their efficacy. In the spellbinding

1 Friedrich Nietzsche, *Beyond Good and Evil* (Walter Kauffman trans.) (New York: Vintage, 1966), p. 52.

symbols of power, in the nocturnal 'experiences' of sacrifice and resignation, in the tarrying with horror and the
faces of monsters, we have already identified some of the
features of that day before yesterday; in *freedom* as decisive, as the justification and guarantee of the strategy for
victory, we identified instead the essential features of the
day after tomorrow. Unlike revolution, which stems from
the internal contradictions of society, overthrown in a precise dialectical relation that corresponds to the 'today', or
at most to the 'tomorrow', revolt conserves from the past
inheritances so heavy as to exclude a genuine dialectic.
In some cases, revolt can be judged politically on a par
with reaction; it is a lost battle and often a serious break
in revolutionary strategy. And yet, precisely because it
excludes the dialectic of the contradictions internal to
capitalism but allows for the violent epiphany of the reactionary components in the hands of the rebels, it conjures
up the 'day after tomorrow'. It conjures up—I say by
analogy with the previous sentence—its *epiphany*. What
relations does that epiphany entertain with historical
reality? To what extent does the epiphany of the 'day after
tomorrow' caused by revolt contribute to the overthrow-
ing of capitalism? The two questions will remain profoundly separate (even if the answer is negative for both)
as long as history is approached in a 'historicist' manner.
From the vantage point of historicism, revolt can be judged
by the more benevolent observer as a well-intentioned but
mistaken representation of the 'day after tomorrow', which
is dangerous and harmful to the revolutionary cause. If the
observer is benevolent but not revolutionary, he will confine himself to speaking of 'an undoubtedly genuine rebellion, even if politically a mishit and historically an error'

(as Mann was reported to have said about the revolt of winter 1918–19). The 'day after tomorrow' invoked by the rebels will have no historical reality. The revolt will not have contributed to the future overthrow of capitalism, because its negative effects will largely offset any possible (if doubtful) classist maturation of the defeated rebels.

At the same time, the revolt will be judged most negatively by those paladins of reaction who are less gifted with political sense. On the one hand, they will refuse its 'reactionary' aspects; on the other, they will not grasp the immediate benefits that it implies for reaction.

We can find instead a possibility of judging the revolt's epiphany of the 'day after tomorrow' in a phenomenological investigation that would proceed from within, granting *from within* objectivity to the revolt and to its experiences of time. This is not simply a question of 'reckoning' with the deplorable or remarkable character of the revolt but of recognizing ('paradoxically'?) in revolt that hyperbole of reaction that prepares the day after tomorrow rather than the revolution. If what counts is only today or tomorrow, there is no action more execrable than revolt. But if the 'day after tomorrow' matters, and matters more than today or tomorrow, revolt is a highly positive fact. In terms of immediate political strategy, it is very difficult to harmonize this point of view with the daily waging of battle. The reason being that revolt is not positive because it *prepares* the day after tomorrow inasmuch as it evokes its advance epiphany (alongside defeat in the present). To anticipate the epiphany of a future time—or even of a future victory— does not mean preparing the day after tomorrow, even if we understand this in terms of the dramatic maturation of class consciousness. Revolt does not favour the maturation of class consciousness. However, in its profoundly bourgeois character, in its hyperbole of the dominants of bourgeois consciousness, revolt constitutes the only effective overcoming of bourgeois society, culture and spirit. An overcoming like that of every hyperbole, which gives birth to its opposite. Socialist revolution partakes of a historical dialectic with the bourgeois world; it contests it concretely, today and tomorrow, but it does not overcome it. Revolt is the hyperbole of the bourgeois world, pushed to the point of its overcoming. The epiphany of today or tomorrow, always joined to the preparation for tomorrow, is the maturation of class consciousness. The epiphany of the day after tomorrow is the maturation of a *human* consciousness, for which it would be limiting to speak of class consciousness.

Because it implies an extremely long-term historical change, revolt rules out a long-term strategy. Revolt is incompatible with revolutionary strategy because it is not the preparation of tomorrow but the parturition of the day after tomorrow. Revolution evaluates with extreme care the possibilities of survival of the rebels—one must be alive tomorrow and then tomorrow and then tomorrow again. Revolt openly defies 'historicist' survival. The one who, better than anyone else, confronted this problem with lucidity, was a potential rebel involved in a revolution: 'I despise the dust that forms me and speaks to you. This dust you may persecute and kill, but I defy you to rob me of that independent life I have given myself in the ages and in the heavens.'[2] Saint-Just *dixit*.

In his essay on eternal return, Mircea Eliade tackles first of all the sufferings that men are burdened with by historical events; not 'the problem of evil, which, from whatever angle it be viewed, remains a philosophical and religious problem' but 'the problem of history as history, of the "evil" that is bound up not with man's condition but with his behaviour.'[3] The study of the epiphanies of the myth of eternal return shows how millions of men have found refuge from the terrors and pains imposed by history by becoming aware of a meta-historical justification for such anguish; and Eliade's participation in these sufferings is so empathetic as to become a methodological norm. Observing that 'Every hero repeated the archetypal gesture, every war rehearsed the struggle between good and evil, every fresh social injustice was identified with the sufferings of the Saviour,' Eliade affirms:

> It is not our part to decide whether such motives were puerile or not, or whether such a refusal of history always proved efficacious. In our opinion, only one fact counts: by virtue of this view, tens of millions of men were able, for century after century, to endure great historical pressures without despairing, without committing suicide or falling into that spiritual aridity that always brings with it a relativistic or nihilistic view of history.[4]

2 Philip Joseph Benjamin Buchez and Prosper Charles Roux eds, *Histoire parlementaire de la révolution française*, VOLS 35–6 (1815), p. 275.

3 Mircea Eliade, *The Myth of the Eternal Return: Or, Cosmos and History* (Princeton, NJ: Princeton University Press, 1971), pp. 149–50.

4 Ibid., pp. 150–1.

The activity of the historian is identified with a plunging down into the human, in which all that counts are the sufferings of men and the moments of respite. Eliade implicitly holds that the true reality of man is to be found in the experiences of pain and joy—not in thought, which is capable of rationally opposing itself to pain by attacking its roots in political action. The myth of eternal return has generally manifested itself as a genuine myth, surfacing spontaneously from the depths of the psyche, and not as a technicized myth, deliberately invoked in the context of political action. In suspending his judgement about the moral goodness of the political consequences of such genuine mythical epiphanies, Eliade limits himself to noting that man suffers, or that he ceases to suffer in the instant of suffering or respite, independently of his future. So he does not see man as the protagonist of his future and that of his descendants but only as the protagonist of the instant of his emotion (we could even say that he regards the instant of emotion as an eternal present also in the sense of the species and not just the individual, as Rilke understood it in the *Duino Elegies*). Moreover, even in the face of man immobilized in the hour of pain or joy, Eliade does not intend to advance a moral judgement—he does not say that it is *good* for man to manage to endure suffering by justifying it with a mythical precedent; he confines himself instead to observing that, through such a justification, man has been able to endure history without suffering too much and thus without becoming spiritually barren. It is evident, however, that this attitude both reproduces and replaces that of the moralist, by proposing as a desirable end not moral *good* but spiritual vitality (the opposite of barrenness), one that consists in the faculty of opening up to myth and in the consequent metaphysical valorization of human existence.

In the historical domain of 'mythological religions', myth does not imply an authentic participation in metaphysics, if we understand by this a direct relationship with the Obscure God, that is, with the unknown divine force which, in the eyes of the modern historian, flickers beyond the horizon of myth. Ancient myth, in the instant that it opened man to the *other*, led him back to himself. But the fate of living outside the great 'mythological religions' forces you to consider your gaze as affected by myopia with regard to the metaphysical horizon dominated by the figure of the Obscure God. By 'fate' we understand the existential norm of the phenomenon of knowledge in which reason participates, a knowledge intrinsically dynamic in accordance with a trajectory framed by the reality of biological becoming.

This trajectory, which led man from the *in me there is thought* to *I think*, is undoubtedly in our thinking a Darwinian inheritance. Towards it, we feel a love-hatred that is manifest in the desire to escape historical time by countering the *historical* trajectory of knowledge with the reference to the Obscure God, conceived as an inevitable consequence of the self-same trajectory. But I do not intend to resolve such an antinomy since I consider it to be intrinsic (whether in this form or some other) to the human will, to emotion and understanding—a double Sophia.

The implication *great pain–spiritual barrenness* is presented by Eliade as obvious—man becomes barren if

history burdens him with immense sufferings for which
he is unable to find justification. From an empirical viewpoint—the only acceptable one in this situation—the
axiom seems broadly true. Even the phenomenon of
Marxism does not jar with such conclusions, if we recall
that Eliade acknowledges the presence in Marxist ideology of a meta-historical justification for the sufferings
imposed on those who fight for progress—he affirms that
Marxism justifies the sufferings of struggle with the faith
in a mythical golden age of social justice, placed not at
the beginning but at the end of historical time. Yet it
appears that, when it comes to Marxism, Eliade leaves
behind the tenets of his phenomenological methodology
by failing to consider the importance attributed by Marxists to provisional and partial conquests of welfare and
social justice. By not considering, in other words, that
though the Marxist revolutionary very often recognizes
the impossibility, both for himself and his successors, of
reaching a golden age, he remains committed to the elimination—be it within narrow limits—of sufferings and
injustices. Even if we were to accept that Marx's writings,
in their radical theoretical structure, propose a vision of
history drawn from the myth of *absolute* progress, we
should not forget in a phenomenological study that the
consciousness of the Marxist activist is generally the
bearer of a mythicizing optimism only at the programmatic level, and that he often perceives with great clarity
the limits, and not only the present ones, of the results of
political action with a progressive social meaning. To
those who would object that such an attitude belongs to
the revisionists within the Marxist field, one could reply
that maximalist Marxism too is constituted not only by

programmatic declarations—which are sometimes formulated in a mythicizing language—but also by the consciousnesses of its followers, who (unlike the prototype of the rebel) very often plainly undertake a struggle whose results are notable even if they are not absolute. Even those who aim to conquer an absolute good generally know that their action, and that of those who come after them, will only achieve partial results. This paradox is a constant of political life, wherein it represents a manifestation of that double Sophia which we've already called upon to justify an antinomy in our discourse. The paradox also becomes more comprehensible once we consider the deformation that the notion of historical time undergoes when myths are absent and the present is so painful as to lead one to see the future as an extreme possibility of salvation. This is how the future of the Marxist *absolute* should be understood—not the extreme future, the golden age, but the day that comes right after today, the day in which *maybe* the pain of today will be transformed into good. A relative good and a relative future— the consciousness of most activists of maximalist Marxism does not escape this limitation.

The eternal present, in which past and future fatefully merge, is the reality implicit in the genuineness of mythical experiences. The time and place of origins—in which the *arché* takes shape—partake of the act in which man attains myth, and they encompass past and future in an existential immobility. These temporal determinations—*past, present, future*, which become *contemporary*—also belong to those who operate 'from outside' on myth; they constitute instruments that are almost incompatible with the reality of the object to which they're applied, as is already attested by the paradox of the 'eternal present'. Noting this incompatibility means, ultimately, taking cognizance of the gravity of the objections raised by many scholars against the use of spatiotemporal determinations with regard to the *surfacing* of mythical images to consciousness. The validity of the intellectual 'model' in which consciousness and the unconscious appear as two places, and mythical epiphany configured as a movement of images from the one to the other, has already been repeatedly questioned. Yet it was Rilke, in proposing the formula 'Who pours forth like a spring is by knowledge herself known,' who resolved the contrast between spatial determinations and the reality of consciousness and the unconscious, recognizing in the *pouring forth* the mode of being characterized by death, which may be spatially and temporally described without taking one's distance from the reality of mythical epiphany. If we then wish to understand the attitude of Eliade, set on participating in the pain and joy of man in the immobile hour of emotion, we need to invoke that religion of death 'alone in the world eternal',[5] from which originates every intuition of the eternal present and the eternal return. *Pouring forth* is destroying oneself in opening up to the reality that discloses itself in emotion. A man still in an hour of emotion, abstracted from historical time, is a man who becomes himself in death, that is, in the instant of his destruction in emotion—a destruction without which the hour of emotion cannot be said to be eternally present. Too often, the great Greek experience of Orphic death

5 Giacomo Leopardi, 'Chorus of the Dead in the Laboratory of Frederick Ruysch' (1824, John Herrington trans.), *The New Criterion* 8 (June 1990): 54.

has been distorted by modern philology with the formula of death-rebirth, with the emphasis especially on rebirth. The experience of death undergone by the devout in Eleusis and Samothrace was a plunging into death—the 'resurrection' of Kore was not a new participation in life, similar to, if more true, than the one prior to death but participation in death 'alone in the world eternal'. If we wish to identify two stages in the Eleusian experience (those traditionally defined as 'death' and 'rebirth'), we must note that we are dealing with two phases of accession to death: the first, in which death is juxtaposed to life as its 'difference'; the second, in which death is revealed as 'eternal present'. The incompatibility between historical time and mythical time thus takes on the features of an antinomy between life and death; but historical time and mythical time, life and death, are connected by an element—man, who partakes in both history and myth.

Eliade's thought can thus be seen to reveal an aspect of the crisis of modern Western humanism, within which the convictions of the humanist Zeitblom in Mann's *Doctor Faustus* ('I often explained to my senior students how culture is actually the reverent, orderly, I may even say, propitiatory inclusion of the nocturnal and the monstrous in the cult of the gods'[6]) shine an ambiguous light on the current possibilities of renewing Jacob Burckhardt's plan:

> Our point of departure will be the only one accessible to us, the only centre of all things: man with his sufferings, his strivings, his works, man as he is, as he has been and as he always will be. We shall study what is recurrent, constant and

6 Mann, *Doctor Faustus*, p. 12.

typical, in the way that it is reflected in us and through us becomes intelligible.[7]

Burckhardt's words already contained the presupposition of the immobility of the 'hour of man', situated by Eliade at the intersection of historical time and mythical time. But Burckhardt's thought involved a pedagogical demand aimed at the tomorrow which is absent from Eliade's essay, just as that need for moral valuation that in Edmund Husserl's work permeates the applications of the phenomenological method is absent from it. And yet Eliade too intends directly to avail himself of phenomenology. In other words, Eliade's humanism is forced to undergo a strong metaphysical pressure at whose origin we do not find Good and Evil but a divinity akin to the Obscure God, as named in the lyrical poetry of Gottfried Benn, or to Nietzsche's Unknown God. It is worth recalling that in Eliade's novel *The Forbidden Forest*, the protagonist Stefan takes shelter from time to time in a secret room, far from his usual dwelling, whose location he does not reveal even to his wife; she is forbidden from entering it.[8] It is a 'Bluebeard's room', as Stefan's wife explicitly puts it; as has been shown by ethnology, of which Eliade is a master, in 'Bluebeard's room', in the 'secret room' of fables, survives the image of the place of initiatory segregation in which neophytes lived through their experience of death. In the novel, the secret room is contiguous

7 Jacob Burckhardt, *Force and Freedom: Reflections on History* (James Hastings Nichols ed.) (New York: Pantheon, 1943), p. 82 (translation modified).

8 Mircea Eliade, *The Forbidden Forest* (Mac Linscott Ricketts and Mary Park Stevenson trans) (Notre Dame, IN: University of Notre Dame Press, 1978).

with everyday life—it is a simple hotel room in Bucharest. It represents a place of death and eternity that is always available during the course of the day. Stefan enters it as he would enter a perennially open tomb or those huts in the woods where the death of the initiated takes place. Just as the initiated return at last to the their dwellings marked by the experience of death, Stefan comes home from the secret room still bearing the traces of his solitary relation with the Beyond—his wife 'glimpsed him from afar and understood from his absent demeanour, from his way of walking, that he had been in the secret room. It seemed to her then that Stefan would definitively regain consciousness only after having spent some time in her arms.'[9]

The image of the secret room in *The Forbidden Forest* is also strongly reminiscent of the room described by Mann in the novella *The Wardrobe*—the boarding-house room in an unknown city in which Albrecht van der Qualen finds, in a wardrobe open onto the Beyond, the mysterious female figure who nearly every night tells him lengthy stories and unites herself with him.[10] The protagonist of *The Wardrobe* is called *van der Qualen*, 'of the ordeals', and the novella could indeed be chosen as the emblem of the human recourse to myth to relieve pain, as discussed by Eliade. In it, Mann has the man 'of the ordeals' act in a state that seems to oscillate between waking and sleep, during which everything seems darkly to allude to mysterious realities which in fact lie 'beyond'.

9 Eliade, *The Forbidden Forest*.
10 Thomas Mann, *The Wardrobe* in *Stories from Three Decades* (Helen Tracy Lowe-Porter trans.) (New York: Alfred A. Knopf, 1936), pp. 71–7.

This state seems to us to belong to man placed exceptionally in the face of a transitory epiphany of the Obscure God—transitory in historical time but coinciding with the immobile hour of mythical time.

In his essay, Eliade distinguishes between two fundamental types of meta-historical justification for historical events: history understood as eternal return, perennially renewing the mythical *arché*; or history as a series of ever new theophanies, in accordance with Judaeo-Christian religious experience. In Jewish religious thought, the Dark God who forms the background for mythologies came to the fore as a force directly acting in history, thereby losing part of his obscurity and almost acquiring a face. The condition of the devout before such a God increasingly approached the waking state and their defence against the sufferings imposed by history expressed itself in the identification of historical time with the 'time of God'. Chased from what Eliade defines as 'the paradise of archetypes', man no longer countered historical time with mythical time and abandoned the immobile hour of myth for the sake of the intimate dynamic of theophanies.

By proposing Christianity as the only religion capable of saving modern man from the pain of history, Eliade is not offering an optimistic message. In his argument, archetypes truly are the 'lost paradise', now foreclosed to men, access to which implied 'a certain metaphysical "valorization" of human existence', which probably amounted to recognizing the human faculty of standing at the crossroads between life and death.[11] However, the appreciation of this faculty in Eliade's essay is especially focused on its

11 Eliade, *The Myth of the Eternal Return*, p. xi.

particular 'openness' towards death and towards the flux of myth—an openness that disappears almost entirely in the the religious world of Judaism and Christianity.

Such a devotion towards death should not be understood as a polemical negation of life; the death that corresponds to self-destruction in emotion, and to the abandonment to the flux of myth, is not the victorious antagonist of life but, rather, the inner space in which man perceives and assumes the perennial elements of his existence. In this way, the time of myth can be said to be the hour of death inasmuch as it represents the eternity with which human being is commingled. It is the deep shelter, the secret room in which the spirit draws on its reality and comes to know the archetypes, the perennial forms capable of harmony between the objective and the subjective. The sufferings imposed by history can make the human spirit barren because they can lead it through despair to see in death only the cessation of life, the great dark enemy of humanity. He who suffers and finds no justification for his suffering is obviously incapable of discovering the deep and authentic face of death; he comes to a stop before the mask of pain with which despair counterfeits the reality of death. A civilization whose relationship with death lies solely under the sign of despair is a civilization close to its end.

A general symptom of the barren relationship with death typical of such a civilization is the great importance it accords to memory. The exercise of memory becomes a struggle against death, the desperate search for a bond with eternity that would have nothing to do with death. Just think of an easily verifiable example—in the modern

Western world, the practice of visiting cemeteries is often motivated by the desire to nourish the memory of the dead. The grave has entirely lost its ancient meaning as a place on the threshold of the Beyond, a point of intersection between the kingdom of the living and the kingdom of the dead, to become nothing more than a spur to memory; the current custom of visiting graves is diametrically opposed to the ancient cult of the dead and the grave is now valorized *in opposition* to death, an aid to memory as the latter fights against death.

Opposed to such a valorization of memory is the attitude of those who still participate in the 'paradise of the archetypes'. Recalling, among others, Raffaele Pettazzoni's studies on the confession of sins, Eliade depicts the abiding desire of primitives to abolish memory insofar as it represents a bond with historical time and thus a bond with pain and with sin. He even asks himself whether,

> in the primitive's desire to have no 'memory,' not to record time, and to content himself with tolerating it simply as a dimension of his existence, but without 'interiorizing' it, without transforming it into consciousness, should we rather see his thirst for the 'ontic,' his will to be, to be after the fashion of the archetypal beings whose gestures he constantly repeats?[12]

In Eliade's argument, this is almost rhetorical, since his positive response already seems implicit in the question. If myth is a structure of self-consciousness, and if it reveals intimate ties with man's vision of inorganic matter, it is legitimate to see in the phenomenon of self-

12 Ibid., p. 91.

consciousness marked by mythical epiphany a knowledge of man about that part of himself which is composed of chemical elements and which comes in that way to be part of the I. Death, the eternal present in which the hour of myth stands still, allows man to interiorize the inorganic matter of which he's composed. Death also presides over the instant in which the inorganic components of man, during and after putrefaction, come apart and form new bonds.

The regeneration of time through the myth of eternal return thus turns into a renewed conquest of innocence; and the participation of consciousness in that regeneration corresponds to the longing for an absolute innocence which primitive man too has lost—the innocence of the being devoid of consciousness, the being who exists without knowing it.

Is revealing these fundamental constants of primitive thought a pedagogical and healing action with respect to one who's already taken his distance from this form of thought? A positive answer is legitimate only if it does not imply in the pedagogue the desire to propose those spiritual experiences as a medicine for contemporary humanity. It would be mistaken—and Eliade is the first to recognize it—to try to heal men today by impelling them towards the vain effort of recovering the thinking of primitive man. The knowledge of the primordial experiences of the human spirit is healing to the extent that it can push contemporary man to recover a deep and fecund relationship with death—a relationship which will certainly not be that of primitive man but which will satisfy a demand that will remain present in man for as long as there will be an inner space of death and eternity in human being.

The knowledge of primordial experiences makes evident the collective character of the regeneration which, for primitive man, took place through the periodic abolition of time. What man draws from his inner space of death is objective and collective, even if the act through which he does this is intimately subjective. With such an act of subjective will, man attains to collectivity and fully realizes his being. An exclusively subjective relation with death and with myth is contrary to the nature of their epiphanies in man. It derives from a deliberate invocatory action which lacks spontaneity and genuineness, doubtless aiming towards a particular purpose. It is, in other words, a technicization of myth in the sense indicated by Kerényi and thus a dangerous and culpable exploitation of the irrational. Modern man must ward off this danger, repeatedly manifest in recent history, by purifying his relations with the irrational from all interest, thereby gaining that waking state that Heraclitus defined as belonging to those who participate in a common world. The relation with death that everyone carries in themselves is not realized in a state of sleep—consciousness must fully partake in the effort of drawing on primordial realities. Consciousness is indeed an organic component of human being and, as such, is intrinsically tied to both life and death. This has often been denied, because the field in which consciousness is exercised is clearly that of historical events; but I don't believe that this is an error caused by the distorted viewpoint of those who treat death simply as the enemy of life. If death is conceived as the inner space of

eternity present in man's existence, it is possible to understand how the usual notion of consciousness illuminated
only one aspect of the phenomenon whereby the I knows
that it is an I. Another aspect of this phenomenon is the
self-consciousness of the I in the instant in which it participates in the harmony between objective and subjective, in
the inner space in which death is the eternal present. We
have described this situation as self-destruction in emotion and as abandonment to the flux of myth. According
to the language of the natural sciences, the participation
of the self-conscious I in its own destruction would
involve a critical point beyond which destruction would
be totally complete and nothing would be left of the I.
But the self-conscious I is not a proper object of life, progressively eroded by death; rather, it is the synthesis of
the element common to life and death, present in the
human being who stands at the crossroads between life
and death. The I, in the moment in which it is conscious
of itself, is also permeated with death, and its sinking into
death continually takes place during what we usually consider to be the life of man. The I therefore knows life and
death, permanence and self-destruction, historical time
and mythical time together. It is the common element,
the point of intersection, between two universes—of life
and historical time; of death and mythical time. Such a
point of contact takes on a paradoxical reality when we
consider that historical time is in constant movement
while mythical time is constant stillness.

A paradoxical reality, however, is not necessarily
false, since the paradox may stem from a simple, ordinary
error of sight, an optical illusion. In the moment that it

gains access to myth, the I that is subject to historical time while nevertheless participating in mythical time, 'pours forth like a spring'; it destroys itself in a dynamic process that involves its historical duration. In other words, the I really participates in the flow of history when it succeeds in identifying history with the course of its own destruction and therefore with its access to myth. In this way, the contrast between the dynamic and the immobile which gives rise to the paradox is resolved and clarified by the description of the 'existential functioning' of the I, which represents the common denominator of the double Sophia.

Fifty years ago, Mann began his *Reflections of a Non-political Man* by confronting his espousal of, as well as his intimate struggle with, Dostoevsky. Taking into account the symmetry of our concerns, I take the liberty of referring to the same writer, the enigmatic Dostoevsky who could be called both a 'subversive' and a 'fierce reactionary'.

Modern culture is far closer to Manichaeanism than the latter's most obvious theological consequences might suggest. Manichaeanism does not simply mean the dogmatic opposition of light and darkness, God and matter; it also means the horror of chaos, the exaggerated dread at the disordered teeming of forms that a famous psalm from Turpan evokes as the special attribute of the Prince of Darkness.[13] The great spiritual crisis at whose peak Goethe's Doctor Faust makes his pact with the Devil is born of recognizing the impossibility not of *dominating*

13 Jesi's reference is to Manicheaen writings originating in Uyghur kingdom of Turpan, in present-day Xinjiang, China. See W. B. Henning, 'The Book of the Giants', *Bulletin of the School of Oriental and African Studies* 11(1) (1943): 52–74. [Trans.]

but of *ordering* the multiform reality of matter. In fact, the only apparent order suggested by alchemy and the esoteric sciences consists in man's acceptance of the intimate disorder of matter as a fundamental law of nature, subdivided into innumerable clauses and codicils. A rational reckoning radically applied to the monster of the thousand faces which, in confronting man, takes on the name of 'nature', can at best result in an autopsy; but the life of the monster is then lost, albeit ready to be reborn, as though Heracles were scrutinizing a recently severed Hydra head while others sprung forth to threaten him. When some great alchemists chose as their emblem Heracles in the act of vanquishing the Nemean lion, they were alluding to domination alone. Manichaean religious experience, on the other hand, is not consumed by the desire for that domination—it does not aim, in other words, to gain sovereignty over the demons; what it manifests is the anguish stemming from the recognition of impossible order.

An argument at whose head stands the name of Dostoevsky can only begin with an encomium to darkness.[14] Of darkness it is almost impossible to speak without composing an encomium or an aretalogy because it is one of the privileged realities for which language only possesses evocative words; an evocation of darkness cannot avoid apologia—even if the evocation comes from one readying himself to confront the epiphany of the enemy—since it does not consist, strictly speaking, in becoming aware but in an experience that involves one's entire being. Such an experience cannot take place

14 *Tenebra*. [Trans.]

without a certain abandonment, a certain acceptance (whence the encomium) of the intimate reality of the thing evoked. Darkness is a word that may seem time-worn—like 'mystery' in times alien to the ritual celebration of genuine mysteries—but, despite the seeming wear, the word conserves its authentic evocative value. Yet the evocation takes place in vain, like the movement of a mechanism isolated from the others, and this does not grant more effective weapons to the summoners who aim defensively to face the summoned reality, because the mechanism turns idly within their very existence, causing imbalances and agonies.

In a sense, this realization is already an encomium to darkness, since observing the uncertainties and pains provoked by its 'idle' epiphany in our psyche—which is incapable of welcoming it and connecting its mechanism to all the other mechanisms of our existence without succumbing to it—is an explicit recognition of the sovereignty and existential necessity of darkness.

Beyond these convoluted words, a true humanist from bygone times would have spoken of our meagre preparation for death. Erasmus' *tristitia* has its roots in that preparation—in which he was certainly our better—and in the recognition of the solitude that fatefully comes to surround the best prepared.

'Meagre preparation for death' is a much clearer proposition, more elegant and meaningful, than the intricate argument we've been making up to now. But we could not have reached it right away, nor could we now limit ourselves to treating it as a precis of our thinking. The bad conscience that forces us to try and clarify the modalities of our relationship with darkness is very much part of that meagre preparation. To sideline that effort and limit ourselves to the epigrammatic phrase would be the sign of real presumption—the aphorism is legitimate for those who advance on firm ground, not for those who struggle in the shadows.

From this point of view, we find ourselves in a favourable situation to understand the behaviour of Dostoevsky; he lived precariously in the (at times desperate) attempt to perfect his preparation for death.

In 1870, while in Dresden, Dostoevsky heard from his brother-in-law I. G. Snitkin the recent story of S. G. Necha-yev, who had organized revolutionary groups among the students of Moscow's Institute of Agronomy, having passed himself off as the agent of People's Retribution (Narodnaya Rasprava), a non-existent secret society. Nechayev had managed to promote subversive initiatives of a nihilist bent with methods that were considered 'criminal', and not just by his enemies. Later, most likely, Dostoevsky learnt from the papers that Nechayev had murdered the student Ivanov after accusing him of treason for not accepting his methods. After fleeing to Switzerland, Nechayev developed close ties with Bakunin and tried to carry on from a distance his terroristic propaganda back home, until he was arrested in 1872 and delivered to the Russian police as a common criminal. Dostoevsky followed his trial; but even before it began, the writer had finished a novel, *Demons*, in which Nechayev's crime occupies a central place as a symbol rooted in the reality of the sins of terrorism which Dostoevsky denounced as the offspring of the Occidentalism and

utopian socialism of Vissarion Belinsky, Timofey Granovsky and the Petrashevsky circle.[15] Pyotr Verkhovensky, who in the novel embodies Nechayev, is in fact the
son of the intellectual Stepan Trofimovich Verkhovensky,
the stand-in for Granovsky, professor of history at University of Moscow and typical Westernizer of the 1840s.

The forms of myth pale when behind them looms the
presence of an obscure and unknown God. Understood
as a religious experience, mythology is incompatible with
devotion to the *deus absconditus*—not so much because it
is difficult to integrate within it a faceless entity (just think
of the mythological Greek notion of non-existence—the
image of Hades) but because the presence of the unknown
God breaks man's spontaneous trust in the truthfulness of
myth, reducing the patrimony of myth to a fatal burden
from which we can expect neither illumination nor salvation. But even when confronted with the *deus absconditus*, myth does not disappear; in the instant in which it
becomes a dark matter, it gains the gravity of a destiny
that inheres in the human organism; a fate of impurity
which in every hour of life continues to hint towards
death.

Those deprived of defences against that fatal force—
those who, like Dostoevsky, are forced to see it penetrate
like a germ of putrefaction and guilt into the very dreams
of a golden age—are destined to see fixed before their
very eyes the image of the human sacrifice that it demands;
they can only escape it in the hours in which faith in the
*deus absconditus* (and certainly not God Himself!) doles

15 Fyodor Dostoevsky, *Demons* (Ronald Meyer ed., Robert A. Maguire
trans. and Robert L. Belknap introd.) (London: Penguin, 2008).

out provisional salvation. From mortified myth, debased to the level of a useless but insuppressible experience of being, only human sacrifice can come—murder or suicide as the consequence of the punishing and purifying drive which leads to the suppression in oneself or others of a perennially renewed guilt, the vain image that always surfaces where there should be nothingness instead. The horror of a proliferation of images generated by a process that coincides with the human experience of the I, of space and time, of images that contaminate every action and every spiritual emotion, is not just difficult to bear by anyone who demands of himself mystical devotion towards the Obscure God but inevitably leads to the impulse to suppress the mechanism from which these images ceaselessly spring, namely, the human organism.

From this vantage point, the murder of the student Ivanov by the nihilist Nechayev, which Dostoevsky drew upon in the genesis of *Demons*, appears as a historical counterpart of Dostoevsky's own mythical suicide. The mythical time that fatefully casts its shadow over historical time gave Dostoevsky the opportunity to be at the same time Ivan Shatov and Pyotr Verkhovensky, victim and sacrificer, horrified spectator of the homicide and advocate of *necessary* killing.

While the points of contact between Shatov and Dostoevsky have been repeatedly noted by scholars, who have identified Slavic messianism as the common denominator between character and narrator, everyone has naturally viewed the figure of Pyotr Verkhovensky-Nechayev as a fierce caricature of Dostoevsky's foes. *Demons* has always been considered the novel of Dostoevsky's 'great anger' against Westernizers and nihilists alike—against the Godless. Yet Nechayev's nihilism, as the thinking that inspires the homicide, coincided with a dominant strain in Dostoevsky's character—the cruel sacrifice of man conceived as the repository of myths, as the eternal mythologist who had to be killed on the altar of the *deus absconditus*, of the God Dostoevsky called 'Christ' and in whose liturgy the supreme act was participation in pain, in the most intolerable pain. Not so much death as killing.

Dostoevsky's abiding interest in cruel crimes, the fact that his three major novels—*Demons, Crime and Punishment, The Brothers Karamazov*—have at their centre a homicide, make evident the significance and the secret echoes that the writer found not just in guilt but also in killing, in homicide. 'Stavogrin's Confession' has its focal point not in the rape but in the suicide of the seduced girl and in Stavogrin's participation in that death. Stavogrin himself must die a suicide, because the fatal chain of killings—of Maria Timofeevna, of his brother, of Shatov, of the wife and son of Shatov, of Liza—led also to the sacrifice of the character who in *Demons* serves as the supreme scapegoat in Dostoevsky's mysticism. The historical figure of Bakunin is far removed from this bloody and secret story. Bakunin's face is simply a mask to be affixed on the scapegoat, though the latter—because the novel is not enough of a sacral act—continues to dwell in Dostoevsky even after the end of *Demons*. What's more, Dostoevsky's Christianity is the dark hour of the robber who dies for his sins (even if he will perhaps be redeemed). Dostoevsky is, in the name of Christ, his own executioner and that of anyone who might be counted as his brother. In the guise of the brother in Christ, Dostoevsky is the implacable murderer because in his eyes every brother must be purified from the tabes of images—of mythical proliferations—germinating from man's own nature, and must therefore be killed so that the kingdom of Heaven may come but without human faces.

It will be objected that Dostoevsky's Christianity is also, or especially, that of the 'Legend of the Grand Inquisitor'. That passage of *The Brothers Karamazov*, in its immediate moral evidence, appears made to measure to lead back into the confines of bad faith and tendentious interpretation every allusion to Dostoevsky's Christianity that departs from the recognition of the purest evangelical doctrine. But we should be on our guard against such a programmatic aim. Dostoevsky's personality was too complex, dark and multifaceted to be labelled in terms of a univocal devotion to the doctrine of Christian love, even when this is intended to single him out for praise. 'Regrettably', the very long hours that in *Demons* Stavogrin spends alone in his room, his eyes open, gazing fixedly at the room's ordinary furnishings—rather than on symbols of transcendence—those hours broken by sleep or drowsiness, in which nothing happens and in which nothing is thought by the character (nor, we may legitimately suppose, by the reader), are the poetic material for the desired nothingness. They are allusions to a state of grace offered in its precariousness as the very object of the narration, confessions of the incapacity, given Stavogrin's nature and fortunes, to draw on the absence of images which is sacred to the *deus absconditus* and thus the prelude to that 'great darkness' that is attainable in death.

This is the negative theology practised by Leverkühn; with relation to the new times, Hans Mayer will be able to observe that 'the God of yesterday has been united with the devil of today'.[16] At the same time, understood as the exclusion of a 'providential' deity from historical time, it is a theology of revolt. Revolt excludes Providence—or providential fatefulness, or the providential consequentiality of iron economic laws—just as it does not *prepare* tomorrow. But what is Nietzsche's epiphany of the 'day after tomorrow' if it is not the confirmation of the essential *untimeliness* of revolt? Revolution prepares the future, revolt evokes it. But there is another fundamental difference—the future of revolution is the tomorrow while that of revolt is the day after tomorrow. Accordingly, we can say that revolution is timely, revolt untimely. The tomorrow is timely because the revolutionaries prepare it. The day after tomorrow is untimely because the rebels do not prepare it—they evoke it. Bakunin would have probably not minded being told that revolution is the refusal of the bourgeoisie while revolt is the hyperbole of the bourgeoisie. He would have drawn from it the legitimate conclusion that revolution builds while revolt destroys.

16 Mayer, *Thomas Mann*, p. 291.

# Appendix 1

*Editorial Synopsis*

This book is not the history of the Spartacist movement and insurrection. The title of the collection in which it is

The first document in this appendix is the 'editorial synopsis' for *Spartakus*, drafted by Jesi for the publisher Silva. The two typewritten pages of the original were included in the author's papers along with the manuscript.

This is followed—as testimony to a thematic nucleus that will find in the definitive version a different and wide-ranging articulation—by two fragments from the first chapter of the initial project, proposed to the publisher under the title *The Bourgeois Tradition*. These were found in a folder containing a variety of materials (and marked in the author's handwriting: *Bachofen*). The original typescripts contain: a page with a sketch of the frontispiece; one with indications about the series and number of volume (the same as the ones in the parcel containing *Spartakus*: 'Myth and Symbol of Modern Germany / A series of texts and studies / edited by Furio Jesi /—3. –'); a third page with an epigram from Dante's *Inferno*, 31, 22–4: 'And he to me: "Because thou peerest forth / Athwart the darkness at too great a distance, / It happens that thou errest in thy fancy.' [From Henry Wadsworth Longfellow's 1867 translation of the *Divine Comedy*.—Trans.]

Finally, we include two outlines for tables of contents whose handwritten originals were kept in the same parcel as the manuscript of *Spartakus*. Despite the seeming discordance, the first corresponds to the definitive version, since it bears the same page numbering as the typescript. The second outline registers a later, abandoned compositional hypothesis, entitled 'The Suspension of Time'.

published (*Myth and Symbol of Modern Germany*) offers a
hint about the volume's content—a study of myths and
symbols, whose subtitle (*The Symbology of Revolt*) indicates the desire to achieve observations of a general character, beyond the specific references to German situations.
As an attempt to offer a dialectical alternative to the historicist explanation of the events, this book continues the
argument in the author's earlier book, *Secret Germany* (the
first volume in the collection). The search for the historical
authenticity of this argument is entrusted, not only to the
close scrutiny of specific documentation but to the inter-
weaving of external events with the inner life of masses and
individuals—a deliberately phenomenological interweav-
ing, in a perspective that aims at both spatial and temporal
breadth. The 'German' character of the events under consideration is studied in light of their European character,
just as the class consciousness that is at stake in them is
studied in the ambit of a vaster human self-consciousness.
In this way, the Spartacist revolt of January 1919 becomes
not an occasional pretext but a phenomenon that reveals
constants and critical elements that can also be connected
to contemporary insurrectionary movements, in an organic
dialectical schema. Consequently, the book's language and

In this variant, Jesi thought of adding three chapters, probably
adapting or redrafting as many essays: 'The Double Bard' ('Il vate
doppio'), devoted to *Double Life* (*Doppelleben*), Gottfried Benn's autobiography, published in the May–June 1968 issue of the journal *Fifteen*
(*Quindici*); 'Myth, the Perpetual Master' ('Il mito padrone di sempre')
which appeared in the journal *Ulisse* in February 1972; 'Thomas Mann,
*Joseph and His Brothers*' ('Thomas Mann, *Giuseppe e i suoi fratelli*'),
already published in the collective volume *The Twentieth-Century German
Novel* (*Il romanzo tedesco del Novecento*) (Turin: Einaudi, 1973), which
was then reprinted in *Materiali mitologici*, pp. 253–71. [Ed.]

method belong more to the category of Thomas Mann's
*Reflections of a Nonpolitical Man*, than to those of traditional
historical essays.

[*The Bourgeois Tradition*]
*Chapter I*
Renunciation and memory are frequent companions. It
is rare for the will that determines renunciation to erase
the memory of the lost object (even when it tries to); we
could even say that the act of renunciation confers a
durable form to what is lost.

Such forms make up *Immensee*. Advancing with a
rigorous and cautious respect for psychology, or better
for the 'stirrings of the soul', Theodor Storm went very
far in the 'delight in renunciation' which governs, for
instance, Fromentin's *Dominique*, placing the perennial
forms of what has been renounced in the domain of artistic creation; extracting from the stirrings of the soul not
a wave of pathos but solid, limpid forms, crystalline furnishings of the past in the space of the present, rather than
constants of painful agitation which render the suffering
of the hour of renunciation enduringly active, as a kind
of corrosive acid.

Here, however, lies a contradiction typical of Storm
and of bourgeois culture more widely. The stream of
painful emotion that springs forth from the void opened
by renunciation is contrasted, as by so many obstacles,
by the forms of the lost objects limpidly possessed in
memory, made still and crystalline by death.

[*The Bourgeois Tradition*]

*Chapter I: The Light–Darkness Dialectic*

We all tend to be on the side of the victors, whether the victory takes place on the battlefields, in the squares, or whether it is a victory in the intimate space, albeit open to the cosmos, of one's own consciousness. To choose a political line thus means having sounded out the future and become convinced that a determinate ideology and a determinate strategy will win, sooner or later. This is the kind of moral opportunism which religious morality introduces into the metaphysical sphere and to which non-religious morality offers, by way of orientation and succour, the certainty that a superior principle—justice, peace, fraternity, the force of life, violence, individualism—will be the final victor.

Today we approach the study—at least within the domain of German culture—of bourgeois society, of its culture, of its traditional experience of values, with the conviction that bourgeois society has been and is in contrast with the superior principle to which we give the name of justice. Considered from this point of view, bourgeois society is headed for a defeat, if what we call justice is an objective rather than a subjective reality: a reality, that is, in which epiphany or evocation is a truthful revealer of future times. To speak not only of future times, but of *final* times, would mean welcoming forms of traditional eschatological language and thus consenting to an amalgam of religious and non-religious morality, metaphysics and history, whose danger we are very attuned to. This is first of all the danger, at the methodological level, of simultaneously using two different fields of reference; more deeply, it is the danger of instrumentally sacrificing the integrity of both fields by operating with metaphysical reservations and prospects in the domain of history. You can be a historian or a mystic; in mythological terms, the alternative is that of Scipio's dream, and only genuine mythology—and not a piece of writing like this essay—permits the simultaneous figuration of opposites.

A critique of the Marxist philosophy of history should emerge precisely from the recognition of this ambiguity and of the poverty of Marxist mythology, from which one would need to deduce that Marxism—beyond a certain Germanism in Marx—gains truth there where it emancipates itself from the pseudo-myth of the golden age of perfect justice so as to limit itself (thereby gaining moral weight) to making true only the tenses of the present and of the 'proximate future'.

[Table of Contents 1]

---

1 These first four chapters are marked by a bracket and question mark in the margins. [Trans.]

[Table of Contents 2]

*Suspension of Time*

## Appendix 2

### THE RIGHT TIME OF REVOLUTION: ROSA LUXEMBURG AND THE PROBLEM OF WORKER'S DEMOCRACY

Revolution, when? The problem of the right time of revolution, as the object of a priori speculation, is not always located at the same juncture in the thinking of the ideologists and strategists of class struggle. Revolution as an action to be prepared, revolutionary situations as historical nodes that must be evaluated with extreme attention and scrutinized in their actuality, constitute in the same way as pre-revolutionary situations—and with no primacy over them—the circle of objects that Marxist ideologists have felt it necessary to keep permanently and globally in focus. The problem of the *sense* of revolution, of its essence-meaning, is perhaps at the centre of this circle. But the problem of the *right time* has been deliberately intertwined with it—so that it too could become central—only by some protagonists of Marxist ideology. Others, beginning with Lenin, have regarded it not only as secondary but as dangerous. From their standpoint, to speculate on the right time of revolution means at the very

Originally published as 'Il giusto tempo della rivoluzione: Rosa Luxemburg e i problemi della democrazia operaia', *Resistenza. Giustizia e libertà* (October 1970): 11–12.

least to run the risk of substituting a prophetic paradigm for the daily appraisal of historical constants, and to base a strategic line upon it. Lenin's assertion is both clear and wilfully relative: there is a revolutionary situation when the dominant classes *can* no longer govern in the old way and the oppressed classes no longer *want* to live in the old way.

In the thinking of Rosa Luxemburg, the problem of the right time enjoys instead a central place, which is all the more recognizable since Luxemburg's thought reveals far more starkly than Lenin's the division between a thought for oneself and a thought for all, individual moral conscience and collective political commitment. Luxemburg and Lenin sought to confront the same problems of tactics and strategy; but in every situation of struggle as in every ideological speculation, Luxemburg dug out from each specific problem another problem: that of the relations between one's own truth and that of others—not only between one's own experiences, one's own language, and others' experiences and languages but especially between one's own ethical predicament and those of others. Destined from very early on to be among the leadership of the proletariat, Luxemburg sensed the risk of any ideological superficiality in the relationships between leadership and mass, party and class; she recognized, in the possible and frequent criticisms against tactical compromises and the scanty collective participation in the elaboration of political activity, only so many blows against the elastic curtain that hid the problem she deemed essential: the problem of the historical possibility of the convergence between, on the one hand, the maturing of

revolutionary situations and, on the other, the translation
in terms of anti-bourgeois strategy of the last great aspi-
ration of the bourgeoisie—the dream of a renewed
humanism. It would be wrong to say that Luxemburg
nurtured excessive hopes in this convergence. But she
was convinced that the maturing of the proletariat's class
consciousness corresponded with an initial phase of the
crisis of bourgeois society; the maturing of class consciousness did not mean, then, the definitive overcoming
of bourgeois ideological conditioning. It was a question
of verifying the degree to and way in which the contents
of the bourgeois worldview, which necessarily flowed
into the initial phase of the emancipation of the proletariat, should be salvaged so that they may not repeat
themselves, or whether the internal contradictions of
bourgeois society repeated themselves in a non-disastrous
manner within the proletariat.

The first of these contradictions was of an ethical
nature. There was the obvious risk of transferring into
the proletariat forms of democracy whose ethical quality
had already profoundly decayed within bourgeois society—the risk, for the proletariat, of counterposing itself
to the bourgeoise as the authentic bearer of democracy,
without managing either to re-inject ethical substance
into traditional democratic institutions or to give expression to new institutions. The crisis of the council system
in Russia showed in hindsight how well-grounded were
Luxemburg's fears, even with respect to a successful revolution. Without particular enthusiasm, but with all the
requisite seriousness, Luxemburg understood that the
proletarian movement had to receive from the most

advanced part of the bourgeoisie the heritage of democracy, and that in so doing it was forced to fill traditional democratic institutions with a genuine moral quality, on pain of the disintegration of the bonds of class consciousness. Only in this way, that is only by restoring moral actuality to some bourgeois institutions (instead of merely countersigning their forms, which is to say their contradictions), could an irremovable bourgeois conditioning be turned against bourgeois society. In this way, the maturing of class consciousness—which was but the initial phase of the emancipation of the proletariat, nourished by originally bourgeois values that the bourgeoisie no longer possessed (namely the value of genuine democracy)—could have given expression to effective weapons in the conquest of power.

The awareness of the difficulties that stood in the way of a more than formal acceptance of the bourgeois democratic heritage—the awareness, that is, of the dangerous ease with which bourgeois democratic institutions could be adopted with the assurance that their moral lacks could be filled by the simple fact of having been taken over by the oppressed class—led Luxemburg to always present the terms of the problem in their rawest form: not only does the political leader of the proletariat have a thought for himself and one for everyone but he often falls into the trap of justifying that ambiguity with tactical motivations and with the mirage of a future in which, having attained the strategic objectives, that dichotomy, which was otherwise deemed inevitable, will automatically be rendered harmless since power will be exercised by the representatives of the 'people'.

For Luxemburg the revolution was not, at least in this sense, a mirage. She did not consider it to be either easy or inevitable, despite being certain that only the revolution, if it took place, could determine the emancipation of the proletariat; above all, she did not consider the revolution as *one* revolutionary action, capable of succeeding once and for all. The proletariat must aim to conquer a hegemonic power and it can only do so through revolution, but the revolution will not be *one* in time, since the maturing of class consciousness corresponds to an initial phase in the crisis of bourgeois society and is necessarily conditioned by the tradition and worldview of the bourgeoisie. The emancipation from bourgeois conditioning, which is the prelude to the *enduring* conquest of power, will only be achieved if the bourgeois heritage—and above all democratic institutions—will be filled by the proletariat with a renewed moral quality, making it possible to turn the weapons of the bourgeoisie against itself, to overcome the antinomy between thinking for oneself and thinking for everyone, life with oneself and life with others. The need for such an overcoming, which constitutes the greatest tension within the effective maturing of class consciousness, ends up translating strategy into tactics; the maturing of consciousness turns into a tactical phase of class struggle insofar as it is subject to inevitable bourgeois conditioning and, with the further maturing of revolutionary situations, to the equally inevitable conditionings of the previously attained phases of emancipation.

Because the revolution cannot be one, once and for all, the possibility of giving oneself and others the least relative answer to the question 'The revolution, when?' depends on the consciousness of the dynamics of the emancipation of the proletariat, understood above all as the process of internal exhaustion of the moral quality granted by the proletariat to bourgeois democratic institutions. This internal exhaustion is viewed by Luxemburg as the source of an interpretation of the opacity of history. We could say that for Luxemburg the I and the others are harried above all by the separation determined by the opacity of future history, and that therefore—since the revolution progressively eliminates that separation— every positive effort to clarify in the least relative terms the impending course of history reduces separation and anxiety; that it puts us in the necessary state of mind to nourish potentially revolutionary forces.

So it's not simply a matter of a bourgeois demand for intellectual honesty but of a necessity made conscious by the conviction that without the clarity—without the truth, as Luxemburg puts it—made possible by the answer to the question about the right time, the I remains partially isolated by history and its pressure from the others, thereby putting a brake on the maturing of revolutionary situations and their outcomes. This is how I think we should understand one of Luxemburg's warnings which has been most trivialized and exploited by counter-revolutionary propaganda, which presents it as an indictment of the praxis of many working-class parties: 'There is nothing so destructive for the revolution as illusions, whereas nothing is of greater use than clear, naked truth'.[1]

1 Rosa Luxemburg, 'Our Program and Political Situation' in *Selected Writings*, p. 393.

It is entirely correct that Luxemburg polemicized harshly against those leaders of the proletariat who thought it necessary to present the masses with satisfactory illusions about the time of revolution and who were so persuaded of the insuperable fatality of the dichotomy between thought for oneself and thought for others that they opted for the solution of erasing their own individual crises by giving form to an apparently monolithic ideology. But Luxemburg did not seek to save her soul with rigorous intellectual honesty. She wanted to use clarity—truth—to bond her I to others, and every I to others, promoting a collective maturing of consciousness which she judged inseparable from the maturing of revolutionary situations and from the possibility for the proletariat to conquer power.

Luxemburg understood perhaps more clearly than every other Marxist ideologist that historical time cannot be limited to the univocally evaluable norm of a sequence of events, but that the only historically *objective* temporal paradigm is the one that stems from the dialectic between the subjective experience of time, proper to single individuals and single groups, and the 'objective' temporal quality of events. Saying the truth meant for her penetrating the global experience of time, which does not exclude any dialectical element, and to ground on that globality the solidarity of multiple individual egos, which alone can bring the right time of revolution near. To establish the right time of revolution is to help to bring it closer. But one cannot seriously answer the question about the right time without simultaneously delving into the experience of those who affirm revolution tomorrow, or today, and into the 'meaning of history' according to which revolution will come when the circumstances permit. Otherwise, we risk worshipping a superhuman 'meaning of history'; denying what Rosa Luxemburg insistently affirmed: that men make their own history.

'The socialist transformation presupposes a long and stubborn struggle in the course of which, quite probably, the proletariat will be repulsed more than once, so that, from the viewpoint of the final outcome of the struggle, it will have necessarily come to power "too early" the first time.'[2] To answer the question about the right time in these terms means, on the one hand, having a global experience of time, which is genuinely objective to the extent that it welcomes the more subjective experiences, allowing them to enrich the otherwise partial notion of a 'meaning of history'; on the other, it entails exercising constant vigilance when it comes to all successful revolutions. Are they really *the* revolution, or rather provisional conquests of power, after which the proletariat will be pushed back by the surviving forces of capitalism or by the victorious proletarian leadership itself? The maturing of class consciousness can make subjective time and 'objective' time increasingly coincide in a single and univocal right time of revolution. But in the revolutions that have been successful up to now has that coincidence been achieved?

This doubt is obviously directed above all towards the Russian revolution, whose success Luxemburg witnessed in the last years of her life. Fifty years later, Lukács

---

2 Rosa Luxemburg, 'Social Reform or Revolution' (Dick Howard trans.), *The Rosa Luxemburg Reader*, pp. 128–67; here, p. 159.

(in the recent interview with the editors of *Der Spiegel*) acknowledged without hesitation the lack of democracy in Russian Communism, recognizing its origin in the political orientation that corresponded to the decisions of Stalin, who would have allowed the doctrine of Trotsky (the unions must be an instrument in support of production) to prevail over that of Lenin (the unions must represent the interests of workers vis-à-vis the bureaucratized state). Lukács dismisses the need for a second October Revolution—with time (10, 20, 30 years), an authentically Soviet system of democratic participation will necessarily come to predominate again in the socialist countries, and it will replace the 'singular, hybrid form, born when Stalin transformed the already precarious remainders of the central councils of workers into a parliament'.[3] These late apologias of the definitive success, despite everything, of the Russian Revolution explicitly underscore the divergence between Luxemburg's thinking and that of Lenin, but also that of Trotsky, when it comes to the evaluation of the political function of unions. Luxemburg stated that unions were involved in the struggle against the *worsening* of the living conditions of workers, recognizing trade unionism as a tactical element that promoted the maturing of consciousness. With Lenin, trade unionism was to become a constant of socialist society; a fundamental constant because it resolved—in its dialectical intervention—the divergence between the time of the first successful revolution and the right time of revolution. Luxemburg's lack of faith in the possibility of this

---

3 ' "Das Ratesystem ist unvermeidlich". Spiegel-Gespräch mit dem Philosophen Georg Lukács', *Der Spiegel* 17 (1970): 153.

function for trade unionism corresponds to her denunciation of any 'realist' acceptance of the break between the bureaucratic socialist state and the labouring class: an acceptance which means treating the first successful revolution as the definitive one, and setting out non-revolutionary correctives—like the dialectical action of trade unionism—to the imperfections of that first revolution. It is easy then to see why in 1925 the executive committee of the Communist International had defined all of Luxemburg's views which diverged from those of Lenin as canonically mistaken and why the accusation of 'spontaneism' would later develop into the characterization of Luxemburgism as a 'syphilitic bacillus' (Ruth Fischer).

With less vehemence, one could speak of a Luxemburgist utopia. But if we contrast that utopia with Lukács's 'realism', which predicts the non-revolutionary and inevitable return of socialist states in a matter of decades to a genuine Soviet system, we think it is possible to see in Luxemburg's thought the more 'realistic' utopia; certainly not as the proclamation of an imminent second October Revolution but as concrete ideological nourishment for revolutionary movements outside Russia. From this point of view too, without a doubt, Luxemburgist thought remains a utopia: but, if nothing else, a utopia which stands apart in its concrete pessimism from the utopias of a revolution which has succeeded once and for all.